# CHRIST
## THROUGH
# MARY

POWERFUL PRAYERS
IN A TIME OF CRISIS

## JANICE T. CONNELL

AUTHOR OF MEETINGS WITH MARY

Christ through Mary: Powerful Prayers in a Time of Crisis

Copyright © 2021 by Janice T. Connell

Published by Four Winds Publishing LLC


Hardcover ISBN: 978-1-7372170-0-8
Paperback ISBN: 978-1-7372170-1-5
eISBN: 978-1-7372170-2-2

Parts of this title were previously published as
*Praying with Mary: A Treasury for All Occasions* in 1997.

# CONTENTS

# PRAYERS

CHAPTER 8

# FOREWORD

God looks for us, each of us. He calls each one by his or her own name, and He finds each of us. He calls every one of us to Himself. No one escapes His call.

God looks for me and for you so effectively, and with such patience and love and determination that, finally, we find Him. And we continue to find Him, and to grow in union with Him. We learn to know Him, speak to Him, be with Him, trust Him, depend on Him.

Here is a book that will help you to find God. Jan Connell was called to write this book that will draw you into intimate prayer to God our Father, to Jesus Christ, to the Holy Spirit, and also to Mary, the Mother of Jesus Christ.

Not of course that we put Mary on the same level with Jesus Christ or the Father or the Holy Spirit. She is not at all, in any way, God or divine any more than you are or I am. But Mary is the Mother of Jesus Christ and, as such, she is, in the order of grace, in the spiritual order, your mother and my mother. Mary helps her children.

Jesus Christ is now and always will be Mary's child. So am I. You are too. We can turn to Mary and obtain her help. She teaches us to find God and know Him more intimately. Mary gently guides us closer to God. She clarifies effective ways for us to avoid sin. She blesses us with God's choice graces that enable us to love more and better.

Mary is transparent, like the air we breathe. She does not let us be centered on her, but always on God. Mary brings us to Him. She is, after all, not just your mother, and my mother. Mary is the Mother of God who has become, in Jesus, human like us in all things except sin. Mary is always and forever the Mother of Jesus Christ who is God, equal to the Father, and one with the Father in the Holy Spirit. We are brothers and sisters of Jesus Christ and children of the Father. And, too, in a different but very real way, we are children of Mary.

Mary has nothing of herself, nothing her own; she wants nothing for herself. She desires everything for her children, for you, for me, and all for the glory of God. Her strength is her nothingness. God has looked and looks still on the lowliness of Mary and she magnifies the Lord and rejoices in Him and helps us to be more consciously united with Him.

Do not be afraid to turn to Mary, or to pray to or with her. She will bring you to the Lord. That is what she does. It is really who she is. We might say that it is her job. It is certainly what Mary wants and can do.

This book will help you find and climb the mountain of peace. It will help you to walk with God. Take your time reading it. When something you read strikes you, stop there. Pause and savor it, let it sink in. Take your time.

Do not race through this book as if it were a book on science or mathematics. What is important in this book is not the information, not the contents; it is not an almanac that you want to use to look up facts. This is a blessed book: what has importance here is not so much the content as the process. Through this book, the Lord wants to teach us the process of climbing the mountain of peace, the way to walk with Him. The "mountain" is the privileged place of encountering God.

Moses met God on the "mountain"; he received the Ten Commandments on Mount Sinai, the holy mountain of God, the special place of His presence. Jesus Christ went up to a mountaintop alone to pray. He called His disciples to the top of a mountain when He chose his twelve Apostles. The transfiguration of Jesus Christ took place on a mountaintop.

The "mountain" is the mountain of peace. *"It shall come to pass in the latter days that the mountain of the house of the LORD shall be established as the highest of the mountains and shall be raised above the hills; and all the nations shall flow to it, and many peoples shall come, and say: Come, let us go up to the mountains of the Lord, to the house of the God of Jacob; that he may teach us his ways and that we may walk in his paths.' For out of Zion shall go forth the law, and the word of the Lord from Jerusalem. He shall judge between the nations and shall decide for many peoples; and they shall beat their swords into plowshares, and their spears into pruning hooks; nation shall not lift up sword against nation, neither shall they learn war anymore"* (Isaiah 2:2–4; *see* Micah 4:1–3).

God leads us to the top of the mountain of peace so that we can find Him there. Value this book. It is one of God's ways of looking for us so that we can find Him always and walk with Him always more closely.

Robert Faricy, S.J., S.T.D.

# INTRODUCTION

## Spiritual Mother Mary

*Christ Through Mary* is about loving our way Home to our Heavenly Father's waiting arms.[1] We need to love and be loved. Mary, Mother of Jesus Christ, was created to bring Divine Love to the love-starved human race.[2] By her graced decision to allow God's Eternal Word to be made flesh and blood of her flesh and blood, she cooperated fully with His Plan for the redemption of the human race.[3] Through Christ, Mary was able to appropriate His divine love into every fiber of her immaculate humanity, not only for herself, but for all of us too.[4] By Mary's faithful obedience to God's Plan, we have full admittance to the Kingdom of Divine Love through Christ if we too cooperate with His Plan.[5]

Scripture identifies Mary, not only as the spiritual mother of the disciples of her Son, but spiritual mother also of the prodigal children of our Heavenly Father.[6] Of course, Christ honors Mary under His own Law.[7] He welcomes His mother's children into His Kingdom of Divine Love.[8] The Lord God formed the immaculate heart of Mary to nurture us His into His Kingdom of Love.[9] Mary's son Jesus Christ is Divine Love Incarnate.[10] Everyone is invited into the maternal safety of Mary's immaculate heart.[11]

As blessings are showered upon their lives, aware Christians love Jesus more profoundly. They learn to speak to Him not only as Lord and Savior, but as their best friend and confidant. When blessings continue to be heaped upon blessings, His unconditional love and goodness draw true believers to classes, theologians, books, and consecrated people. The joy of knowing Him creates a longing to know Him better, to follow Him more perfectly. But lurking in the background are also painful circumstances all people experience that test their faith in Divine Love Incarnate.

Who could have predicted a global pandemic in 2020? Who really foresaw the horror of 09/11 and its consequences for the world? When a close relative or friend is diagnosed with a terminal illness, endures great suffering and dies, family and colleagues are often numb with grief and shock. Few words comfort anyone.

During difficult times that challenge the very depths of human faith, and even in good times, our relationship with the Lord may become what the experts call a "dark night of the soul". Though faith assures us He is with us, Jesus Christ is sometimes so silent, so unreachable that He may as well not be there. When prayer seems to go into an empty box, there are no consolations anywhere. At such times, lonely, naked faith holds our interior life together. In those dark, difficult, desperate moments, severely tested believers need to find the Lord Jesus Christ and have a word with Him. His mother Mary is an amazing resource at such times.[12] Millions of believers, though they pray to God, also pray to Mary for as many reasons as every human ever created.[13]

Those fortunate enough to have open hearts experience an inward answer to any crisis of faith.[14] Those who do not truly know the Lord Jesus Christ as identified in the Nicene Creed

". . . *God from God, Light from Light, true God from true God, begotten not made, one in being with the Father. Through Him all things were made. For us and for our salvation he came down from heaven: by the power of the Holy Spirit, he became incarnate from the Virgin Mary, and was made man....*" eventually discover that fervent, faithful, consistent, seeking, persevering prayer reveals the Lord Jesus Christ as He desires for them at that moment.[15] Faith tells us we all continue to grow and develop forever. There are no static moments in the spiritual realms.

Consider the prophetic dream of a believer from long ago as a personal invitation to climb higher on the mountain of peace now.

"I was living in Biblical times when Jesus walked the earth. My heart was filled with that detachment we hear about from the great spiritual teachers. Jesus Christ was everything to me. He lived in all my thoughts, hopes, goals. His Word was my life's road map, the only language I wanted to understand. I saw myself walking with Him. He was Divine Love Incarnate and I was part of it. Never had I known such ecstatic joy. I knew then why Apostle Peter wanted to build a tent on the Mountain of Transfiguration.[16] I saw Moses, and Elijah too, in the dream. They were filled with the divine love, the rapturous joy flowing from Jesus Christ. I really have no words to explain the experience except to say that a hymn began to resonate in my heart. I recognized that the blades of grass upon which we walked and each of us are one in the divine love of Jesus Christ. All creation and we are one in His divine love. All creation is one with Christ in praising and adoring God. My being was so full of love that, for only a moment, it seemed I melted into all creation through, for, with, and in Jesus Christ.

"Suddenly, the hymn was no longer in my soul and Jesus and I were walking alone. At that moment, He was a strong, determined man with a mission and a destination. There was no numinous splendor now. The scenery was not lush and beautiful. Rather, the area was arid, parched. The high grasses looked heavy in the oppressive heat of a desert summer. Jesus began walking faster than I could possibly manage. I saw in the distance that He turned into a glen hidden behind some tall cedar trees. Following Him, I entered a small shelter protected from the heat of the sun that contained a wooden table and several simple seats. His mother Mary was seated on one of them. Standing beside Mary, Jesus pointed toward me as He said to His Mother, 'Here - prepare this follower of Mine to dine at our table.' Then Jesus quickly turned and walked away. I was devastated. Part of me was dying.

Eternal Truth showed me that to lose the Presence of Jesus Christ is to be extinguished.

"I slowly realized that Mary was looking at me. I knew she could read my heart and my thoughts. I also knew she could feel my abject sorrow. In the blink of an eye, I understood the words of the hymn that once again flooded my being. *'Praise the Holy Trinity. Undivided Unity. Holy God. Mighty God. God Immortal, be adored!'* And in that instant, I knew (on a level that includes the intellect but is not restricted to it) the Lord Jesus Christ as God, the Second Person of the Holy Trinity made flesh in the womb of the Blessed Virgin Mary, and Jesus, the glorified man, *'. . . one in being with the Father, through whom all things are made, God from God, Light from Light, True God from True God . .',* and true man, son of Mary, one Person with two natures, Divine and human. In that moment of graced understanding, I experienced the unconditional love of the Blessed Mother of the Lord Jesus Christ for me, and for all people of all times and places.

The Lord allowed me to know how Mary has been assigned from all eternity to lovingly nurture each of us into the depths of Divine Love. In those graced moments, I received what the spiritual masters refer to as a 'new heart'. Scripture assures us that is His Plan for everyone."[17]

Whether we know Jesus Christ or His mother by name, we all seek them in the depths of our longings, and we need them to reach the heights of our destiny. Faith assures us they are always here for us. We humans are one family. Each of us is a prodigal child of our Heavenly Father redeemed at great price. Our destiny is to respond to divine grace as best we can and accept the redemption obtained for us by Christ through Mary.

Mother Mary knows how to lovingly help each of us respond courageously to God's sometimes terrifying grace. Christ, the Good Shepherd, is sending His mother Mary to our Heavenly Father's prodigal children all over the world in these times to prepare everyone for the Wedding Feast of the Lamb. It is not a coincidence that now you have this information.

Mary is not, nor has she ever been divine. Every grace Mary possesses is a gift from God for her and for us. During the thirty years of silence that preceded His public life, Jesus Christ allowed His Blessed Mother Mary to love, nurture, and serve Him. Yet all the while, God was loving, serving, and nurturing Mary. The relationship of Jesus Christ and His mortal mother Mary is a hint of the mystery of reciprocal divine love and human love. The love flowing between Jesus Christ and His mother Mary is the prototype of the love flowing between God and humanity. Mother Mary, the humblest of all God's creatures, can help us enter quickly and safely into that most exquisite reciprocity of love. Consider a suggested prayer:

O Most Holy Spirit, flowing forth from God the Father and God the Son, guard us and guide us in all our ways…

Mary, full of grace, is able to make our earth journey easier. Mother of the Christ Form within our souls, Mary longs to tenderly hold us close as we travel earth's treacherous paths.[18] Because virtue untested is merely theory, our journey on earth is necessarily challenging.[19] Mary lovingly watches over us and if we allow her to do so, she gently and tenderly nurtures us into focused awareness of God's presence, essence and power in us, around us, and always with us. [20]

The best of mothers, Mary lovingly drinks the bitterest dregs of our cup of sorrow herself.[21] Gentle Mother Mary picks us up when we are needy and silently carries us into the depths of Jesus Christ's divine, all-healing love.[22] In those depths, our entire being is infused with divine peace that passes all understanding.[23]

Because Mary is our heavenly assigned spiritual mother, she rightfully presents our wounded souls, swaddled in her own highly tested virtues, to Jesus Christ in her own stainless hands.[24] As divinely created Mother of God who understands God's Plan as no other human, the Lord answers our prayers with and through Mary, often in ways that transcend the heights of human desire.[25]

The hallowed prayers gathered in this book come from spiritual masters and respected notables. Many of the prayers are archaic but there is charm and grace in their antiquity. Each prayer is a light, a beacon that illumines the glories of God planted in human-kind and our eternal destiny with Christ through Mary.[26] Some of these prayers have sustained our ancestors during countless generations. There is universal hunger to reclaim and participate in the blessings they bring.[27]

People all over the world are awakening to the extraordinary graces flowing from the Holy Rosary, or they need a special prayer in a time of personal, family or global crisis. This book can be used in whatever way feels right. Some will read it from beginning to end in sequence, perhaps savoring favorite stories or prayers they recognize. Others will go directly to the chapter that suits their particular need at the time. Some may simply put this book in a special place for protection, or for use in an emergency.

For countless centuries, prayer has acknowledged the inherent dignity God bestows upon humanity.[28] If you've never consciously prayed before, or it's been quite some time since you've prayed, the very fact that you have this book is your call to come closer to the Lord. Christ is inviting you into intimacy with His family.[29] He wants you to know and trust His Blessed Mother Mary.[30] Those who desire to dwell with Jesus Christ in His Home in Heaven are wise and deeply graced to draw near His Mother now as the opportunity presents itself.

Consider finding a quiet place of solitude. As you hold this book, ask the Lord to reveal to you whatever your deepest need is right now. Then find a prayer that for any reason seems the right one for you. Read it silently or aloud once or many times. Keep this book beside your bed and pray from it every day. Carry it with you when you are far from home. Hold it in times of sorrow or confusion or difficulty or sickness or fear. Download this book so that it is available whenever the need arises. Follow whatever your heart tells you.

If it seems that you do not receive exactly what you ask for in prayer, know for certain that the Lord will give you something better.[31] God answers all prayer.[32] Trust Him. Our Heavenly Father can never be outdone in generosity.[33] His grace is sufficient and overflowing for all who seek Him.[34]

There are many ways to journey Home to our Heavenly Father, perhaps as many as every human ever created.[35] Pray as best you can. In your kindness, mercifully forgive the limitations of this book. If even one of the prayers helps a soul to belong to Christ through Mary, it has done much. Jesus Christ, Divine Mercy Incarnate, redeems souls. We are but servants of the Lord of Hosts privileged beyond our capacities to belong to Divine Love. Christ carries all of us into the reciprocity of love within the Most Holy Trinity. That "FORCE" fulfills the longings of all creation.

Humble like the Magi who followed the Star to Bethlehem, allow Mother Mary and her Infant Christ Child to care for your wounded soul now.[36] Jesus, on Calvary, offered our wounds subsumed within His to God so that His power and wisdom would protect and guide us Home to our Heavenly Father. Our courage to stand firm with Jesus at Calvary flows from Christ through Mary, Our Lady of Golgotha, who is our Mother Most Faithful now and for all eternity. The power of Christ's resurrection is our assurance of our own resurrection from the dead clothed in the splendor of love, justice and peace. We reap what we sow. Loyal to Christ through Mary, we watch and pray always for the glory of God in Christ our Savior.[37] May God bless us all.

## CHAPTER I

# Mother of God

*Prayers of Early Believers*

Have you noticed that human beings are born with broken hearts and wounded souls? Divine love is the only way to heal our deepest needs and longings. Divine love flows from God, and all love, even the feeblest, flows back to God. We need that divine love to live. Nothing else satisfies us. By its very nature, divine love is unconditional. Anything less is mere conditional love which tells us that we are not intrinsically worthy of being loved as we are. Divine Love, however, loved us into being, lovingly sustains us in being, and patiently awaits our reciprocal love.

Each of us was breathed out of the Heart of Divine Love into our mother's womb. If we follow our deepest longings, they will lead us back to the Heart of God Who is Divine Love.[1] Nothing in life is worth so much as reunion with Divine Love. Once that numinous gift is ours, even if only for a moment, we possess conscious awareness of the eternal value of our life and destiny.

Divine Love generates pure grace. Grace, God's infinite love for a human soul, is something no one can earn. No one can buy it either, or deserve it, because God's infinite love is not about deserving. The fact that we exist is proof that we are unconditionally loved forever. Our Heavenly Father created and sustains us on this earth because of His faith in us and His hope that each of us will freely respond to His infinite love by loving our way back Home to His Heart whence we came.

Following Jesus Christ through Mary is a tradition as old as Christianity itself. Saint Joseph learned from the Archangel Gabriel to bond with Jesus Christ through Mary.[2] Saint Elizabeth of the Visitation and her unborn son, Saint John the Baptist, acknowledged unborn Jesus Christ through Mary.[3] Their example is a Lighthouse for all times.

Jesus certainly prayed with His Mother, as did the Apostles. On the night of Pentecost, Mary was present with Jesus Christ's disciples as the group prayed and experienced the Holy Spirit.[4] Sacred scripture offers us a perfect example of Mary's intercessory power in Saint John's scene of the wedding feast at Cana. Although Jesus Christ said to His Mother that His hour for performing public miracles had not yet arrived, Mary, knowing that the hosts would need more wine, simply pointed to her Son and told the wedding attendants, *"Do whatever He tells you."* Jesus Christ, of course, went on to perform a miracle of love, changing the water to wine. Mary's faith in Christ's divine love for each redeemed child of our Heavenly Father was, and always is, unequivocal. Those who invite Mary into their lives find that she lovingly presents our needs and requests to her Son Jesus Christ with perfect faith, realized hope, unlimited compassion and unconditional love for Him and for each of us.

Those who seek a full prayer life appreciate sacred tradition that tells the story of Mary's Dormition. Esteemed Father of the Church, Saint John Damascene wrote about it early in the eighth century:

> "It has been handed down to us from of old, that at the time of the glorious passing of Our Lady, all the Holy Apostles who were then toiling in various parts of the world for the salvation of mankind were in an instant caught up into the air and borne together to Jerusalem. There a vision of angels appeared to them, and they heard the Chant of Angelic Powers. And thus, with glory to God, she yielded up her blessed soul into the hands of her Maker. As for her body, which in an ineffable manner had harbored God, it was carried out for burial amid the hymns of angels and the apostles, and was laid in a tomb at Gethsemane, and for three days the songs of angels continued without ceasing. At the end of the three days the melody of the angels ceased, and Thomas, who alone had been absent, having come on the third day, and desiring to pay homage to that body which had harbored God, the apostles

opened the tomb, but search as they would, nowhere could they discover the sacred body. They found only the clothes in which it had been enshrouded and being refreshed with the ineffable fragrance which proceeded from them, they once more closed the tomb. Astounded at the extraordinary and mysterious event, they could but conclude, that He Whom it had pleased to take flesh of the Virgin Mary, and of her to be made Man and to be born—though He was God the Word and the Lord of glory—and Who had kept her virginity unimpaired even after childbirth, had also been pleased, upon her departure hence, to shield her sinless body from decay, and to honor it by removal hence from the common and universal resurrection."

According to Holy Land lore, one of the most important and beloved prayers to Mary is a significant part of that resplendent scene. Legend tells us that Mary appeared to the apostles gathered there, surrounded by brilliant light and angels of celestial majesty. She wore a crown of twelve stars that seemed to join heaven and earth. The awestruck mourners rejoiced as divine light illumined their human understanding. Filled with the Holy Spirit, they greeted Mother Mary with the following salutation:

*Hail Mary, full of grace, the Lord is with thee. Blessed art thou amongst women and blessed is the fruit of thy womb, Jesus. Holy Mary, Mother of God, pray for us sinners, now and at the hour of our death.*

This prayer, sometimes called the "angelic-apostolic salutation," is the famous *Hail Mary*. It can be prayed on its own but also frequently makes up a part of other prayers, such as the Angelus (this chapter) and, of course, the Holy Rosary (chapter 9).

Early believers knew about and understood the importance of Mary's apparition to the apostles and disciples. No one doubted that Mary lives on in her Son Jesus, the Resurrected Christ. And so, it was only natural that people of faith would begin to spend time each day in prayer with Mother Mary.

Effectively holding the hem of their Heavenly Mother's dress through Marian prayer, people began to climb the spiritual staircase out of human helplessness, poverty, defeat, sickness, and even death. People of all cultures—rulers, nobles, merchants, peasants, and citizens—found solace in Mother Mary's tender compassion. Early Church Fathers and Doctors such as Saints Irenaeus, Epiphanius, Ambrose, Jerome and Augustine taught that our spiritual regeneration is rooted in our relationship to Mary.[5] They themselves prayed to her as most loving, most faithful, most gracious, most grace filled heavenly mother of Jesus Christ the Savior.

Mary continuously nurtures us in the sacred silence of our sanctified longings, gently awakening us more and more to personal awareness of the essence and power of omnipresent God who is Divine Love. Although early prayers with and to Mother Mary come to us from antiquity, each one attests to truths about her loving help and ability to protect, enrich, and care for us today. In this chapter are gathered some wonder-filled prayers to Mother Mary by spiritual masters. As you pray them, you may discover these prayers to Mother Mary are sanctifying beyond telling.

The *Hail Mary Prayer* is beloved throughout the world. Its origins are rooted in the words of the Archangel Gabriel to Mary at the Annunciation and of Elizabeth at the Visitation. Saint Jerome (A.D. 411), Doctor of the Church said the truths contained in the *Hail Mary* are so sublime, so amazing that no human being or angel can fully understand them. Even quarterbacks of would-be championship football teams throw "Hail Mary" passes with high hopes that Saint Jerome is correct.

## THE HAIL MARY PRAYER

Hail Mary, full of grace, the Lord is with thee.
Blessed art thou amongst women and
blessed is the fruit of thy womb, Jesus.
Holy Mary, Mother of God, pray for us sinners,
now and at the hour of our death. Amen.

## THE HAIL MARY
## BYZANTINE RITE PRAYER

Hail, Mother of God, Virgin Mary, full of
grace, the Lord is with you; blessed are you
among women, and blessed is the fruit of your
womb. For you have borne Christ, the Savior
and Deliverer of our souls. Amen.

A prayer and custom from the early days of Christianity continue
throughout the world. Church bells ring out at 6:00 A.M., at
noon, and at 6:00 P.M., reminding people to pray the Angelus.

## THE ANGELUS

The Angel of the Lord declared unto Mary.
And she conceived by the Holy Spirit.
*Pray the Hail Mary.*

Behold the servant of the Lord.
May it be done unto me according to thy Word.
*Pray the Hail Mary.*

And the Word was made flesh
And dwelt amongst us.
*Pray the Hail Mary.*

Pray for us, O Holy Mother of God

That we may be made worthy of the promises of Christ.

Let Us Pray

Pour forth, we beseech Thee, O Lord, Thy grace into
our hearts, that we, to whom the Incarnation
of Christ, Thy Son, was made known by the
message of an angel, may by His passion and cross,
be brought to the glory of His Resurrection. We ask
this through the same Christ our Lord. Amen. [6]

## THE MIRACLE PRAYER

Since at least the third century, the faithful have invoked the
following prayer in times of need. The prayer possibly dates to
the actual time of Christ and may have been spoken directly
to Mary during her life on earth. This prayer is extraordinarily
effective. It is lovingly known as "The Miracle Prayer" because
it has never been known to fail.

### MEMORARE

Remember O most gracious Virgin Mary,
   that never was it known that anyone who fled
   to thy protection, implored thy help,
   or sought thine intercession, was left unaided.

Inspired by this confidence, I fly unto thee
  O Virgin of Virgins, my Mother,
  To thee do I come, before thee I stand,
  sinful and sorrowful.
O Mother of the Word Incarnate, despise not my
petitions, but in thy mercy, hear and answer me.
Amen.

Saint Ephraim (c. 306–373), a revered Doctor of the Church, was never ordained to the priesthood, though he received Holy Orders as a Deacon. So sublime were his prayers and revelations of God's loving Plan for humankind that he is known as the Harp of the Holy Spirit.

O Virgin Immaculate, Mother of God and my
Mother, from your sublime heights turn your eyes
of pity upon me. Filled with confidence in your goodness and knowing full well your power, I beg you to
extend to me your assistance in the journey of life,
which is so full of dangers for my soul. In order that I
may never be a slave of the devil through sin, but may
ever live with my heart humble and pure, I entrust
myself wholly to you. I consecrate my heart to you
forever, my only desire being to love your divine Son,

Jesus. Mary, none of your devout servants has ever perished; may I, too, be saved. Amen.

*Saint Ephraim of Edessa*

Saint John Chrysostom (c. 347–407), an early Father and Doctor of the Church was gifted with immense celestial wisdom and is considered the greatest of the Greek Fathers. He bequeathed us this magnificent prayer.

Would that you know how far our Mother Mary surpasses in dignity the citizens of Heaven. They with fear and trembling stand before God covering their faces with their wings; she offers up the human race to Him to Whom she gave birth. Through her, we may obtain pardon for our sins. Hail then, O Mother, heavenly being, Virgin- throne of God, the glory and bulwark of the Church; pray for us constantly to Jesus your Son, our Lord, that through you, we may find mercy in the day of judgment, and attain to the good things laid up for those who love God.

*Saint John Chrysostom*

The conversion writings of Saint Augustine (c. 354–430) rank among the greatest spiritual literature of all times. A privileged philanderer, young Augustine set out to taste the earth's finest pleasures. At the height of his journey, he heard a voice direct him to read the scriptures with special attention to Romans 13:13–14. The Sacred Word so touched him that he abandoned his former way of life and thereafter sought sanctity more zealously than he had pursued youthful hedonism. Saint Augustine is regarded as one of the most esteemed early Fathers of the Church and is known as the Doctor of God's Grace.

O Blessed Mary, who can return to you sufficient
thanks, or adequately celebrate your praises, for
having by your consent succored a ruined world?
What praise can human weakness offer to you,
which by your means has found the port of salvation?
. . . Holy Mary! succor the miserable, help
the fainthearted, comfort the mournful, pray for
the people, intercede for consecrated souls, pray
for devoted souls and let everyone experience your
intercession who celebrates you. Amen.

*Saint Augustine*

Saint Cyril of Alexandria (c. 376–444) celestially gifted Marian Theologian, Father and Doctor of the Church, presided at the Council of Ephesus, at which the Dogma of Mary, Mother of God was officially proclaimed.

Hail, Mother and Virgin, Eternal Temple of the Godhead, Venerable Treasure of Creation, crown of virginity, support of the true faith, on which the Church is founded throughout the whole world.

Mother of God, who contained the Infinite God under your heart, whom no space can contain: through you the Most Holy Trinity is revealed, adored and glorified, demons are vanquished, Satan cast down from heaven into hell and our fallen nature again assumed into heaven.

Through you the human race, held captive in the bonds of idolatry, arrives at the knowledge of Truth. What more shall I say of you? Hail Mary, through whom kings' rule, through whom the Only begotten Son of God has become the Star of Light to those sitting in darkness and in the shadow of death. Amen.

*Saint Cyril of Alexander*

The following Cradle Song of the Virgin reveals Mother Mary's tender reciprocal love for God and creation that forever changes our relationship with our Creator and His earth. The patriarchs and prophets sought and prayed and dreamed and spoke of that reciprocal love relationship.

Angels! ye holy
Who fly through the palm groves,
Hold quiet the branches,
My Baby is asleep.

Palm-groves of Bethlehem
That sway in the tempest,
the winds are loud moaning
As through you they sweep;
Restrain your wild fury,
Move gently above us;
Hold quiet your branches,
My Baby is asleep.

My Child, my divine One,
Who came down from Heaven,
What pangs He must suffer!
What tears He must weep!
O let Him one moment
Forget all His anguish,

Hold quiet your branches,
My Baby is asleep.

The tempests blow 'round Him;
Ye see that I have not
Wherewith from My Darling
The cold blasts to keep.
O angels, ye holy,
Who o'er us are flying,
Hold quiet the branches—
My Baby is asleep.[7]

## CHAPTER 2

# MOTHER OF DIVINE GRACE

*Prayers of Praise and Gratitude*

Heavenly favors flow to earth from the prayers collected in this chapter that are devoted to praising God with the help of Mary. To praise God with or through Mary is to praise the way God chose to redeem the human race. Most humble of all God's creatures, Mary helps us understand that all praise, honor and glory to God by any creature, herself included, are in fact, God's love flowing through, with, and in Christ our Redeemer. We all profit eternally from that ancient wisdom in prayers of this chapter.

The call to praise, honor and glorify God through Mary is actually Christ's love in us humbly flowing through immaculate Mary to the heights of the Most Holy Trinity. Our prayer with or through Mary is a most humble way of cultivating soul healing gratitude for everything.

We are immortal spiritual beings temporally dwelling in corruptible human bodies who live together all over a planet that seems far from our real Home. We all share equal dignity and value in the Plan of God for humanity. We plod along the earth for a mere 100 years or less enlivened by Divine Love for divine purposes few of us really comprehend.

All of us carry within ourselves unique, exquisite and mysterious gifts from God, including but not limited to our joys, sorrows, families, work, relationships, successes and failures, pain, elation, recreation, disabilities and triumphs. We use these gifts improperly when we don't offer God our thankfulness in a spirit of humble acknowledgement of His Plan.

Created in the Mind of God before the earth began, Mary is the fully human mother of the Unknown God we all seek, yet we undoubtedly know and long to know better and better in our deepest depths.[1] Never tainted by human corruption, Mary is clothed with the merits of God's only begotten Son, Jesus the Christ who incarnated through her, for her and for all of us.[2]

We are temporary stewards of all we possess or seek. Those who live comfortably or have fulfilling lives or satisfying opportunities dare not sink into complacency. Instead, from those with much, much is needed by everyone, and is expected of them by the Lord.

In the widest sense, each gift we have belongs to everyone on this small planet, especially to those who do not yet possess such blessings. Awareness requires us to acknowledge the Lord as our Gift-Giver and praise and thank Him for entrusting us with His gifts, even those we find most challenging. As the great spiritual masters have taught us through the ages, the least among us may in truth be the greatest while those perceived to be the greatest may not be great at all.

God's Son, Jesus the Christ reveals humble Mary to those whom He loves.[3] In her immaculate heart every human longing bears sweet fruit for His Eternal Kingdom of Divine Love. We bring God joy when we humbly praise and thank Him for, with and through Mary. In that way, even our meagerest prayer of praise and thanksgiving releases God's joy somewhere.[4]

The tiny, Scriptural fragment of Mary's earth life teaches us that it is pleasing to God when we use and share His gifts with love, gratitude, obedience, assistance to and petitions for one another. Mary uniquely offers everything she touches to God for His greatest honor and glory.[5]

Sacred tradition teaches us to pray and praise Mother Mary for no other human is closer to God than she, and no one can present our prayer and praise to Jesus Christ, our Heavenly Father and the Holy Spirit more perfectly. In Heaven with Christ, Mother Mary always offers our imperfect prayer and praise to God mingled with the humble merits of her perfected love, thanksgiving, and obedience to His will.

God's love for us and Mother Mary's celestial glory shine in His Plan for the human race. This Plan, which no one fully comprehends, often seems wholly hidden to our human minds. The Lord's Plan for each individual life manifests itself only in God's ways and in God's time. Sometimes, as part of His Plan, difficult situations or events seem overwhelming. But even when they do, when we feel abandoned, betrayed, or unloved, Mother

Mary's example leads us to trust and praise God for His Son, Jesus Christ, our Redeemer who came to us through Mary's faith-filled obedience to the will of God.

Sometimes it is almost impossible to say "thank you" when everything seems wrong. But if we have already practiced faith-filled trusting and praising God in good times for the good things we have, offering prayers of trust and praise in bad times becomes easier. And in all times, good, bad, and uncertain, those who praise God through and with Mary praise the perfectly humble human mother whose Son is hypostatically one of three hypostases of the Holy Trinity.

Mother Mary's humility nourishes our souls into union with the Most Holy Trinity. Her son Jesus the Christ is the Savior of the World, the Risen Redeemer whose name is True Love Incarnate. True love, by its very nature, is reciprocal love. The humble understand shreds of the reciprocity of Divine Love and humankind twinkling in the mystery of thrice Holy Mary, daughter of the Father, Mother of the Son, Spouse of the Holy Spirit, worthy Queen Mother of Heaven and earth.[6]

Jesus Christ quenches our burning thirst for meaning. His loving mercy, so ancient and so new, honors those who honor His mother Mary for God can never be outdone in graciousness.

The following Prayer of the Angel of Peace was brought to earth by a luminous Angel who identified himself as the Guardian Angel of Portugal in 1916. This celestial being appeared three times to three tiny shepherd children, Saint Jacinta, Saint Francisco, and Servant of God Lucia, at Fátima, Portugal. The mysterious Angel of Peace requested the tiny visionaries to make this prayer known globally. Shortly thereafter, Christ's Mother Mary appeared to the children and encouraged them to share this prayer. The tiny visionaries of Fátima lost all sense of earthly time as they prayed this numinous prayer.

O Most Holy Trinity,
Father, Son and Holy Spirit,
I adore Thee profoundly.
I offer Thee the Most Precious
Body, Blood, Soul and Divinity
Of Jesus Christ, present in all
The Tabernacles of the world,
In atonement for the outrages,
Sacrileges and indifference by which
He is grieved.
By the infinite merits of
The most Sacred Heart of Jesus
And the intercession of the Immaculate Heart of Mary,
I beg the conversion of poor sinners. Amen.

Dominican Saint Catherine of Siena, a stigmatist and Doctor of the Church, was born on the feast of the Annunciation in 1347

and lived only thirty-three years. Her relationship with Mary is steeped in celestial wisdom and illumines Mary's sublime place in the human family. Her prayer explains.

If I consider your own great counsel, eternal Trinity,
I see that in your light you saw the dignity and
      nobility of the human race.
So, just as love compelled you to draw us out of
      yourself,
so that same love compelled you to buy us back
      when we were lost.
In fact, you showed that you loved us before we
      existed,
when you chose to draw us out of yourself only for
      love.
But you have shown us greater love still by giving
      us yourself,
shutting yourself up today in the pouch of our
      humanity.
And what more could you have given us
than to give us your very self?
So, you can truly ask us,
"What should I or could I have done for you that
      I have not done?"
I see, then, that whatever your wisdom saw,
in that great eternal council of yours,

as best for our salvation,

is what your mercy willed,

and what your power has today accomplished.

So, in that council, your power, your wisdom, and
    your mercy
        agreed on our salvation

O eternal Trinity.

In that council, your great mercy

chose to be merciful to your creature,

and you, O eternal Trinity, chose to fulfill your
    truth in us

by giving us eternal life.

For this you had created us, that we might share

and be glad in you.

But your justice disagreed with this, protesting in
    the great council

that justice, which lasts forever,

is just as much your hallmark as is mercy.

Therefore, since your justice leaves no evil
    unpunished

nor any good unrewarded,

we could not be saved

because we could not make satisfaction to you for
    our sin.

So, what do you do?

What way did your eternal, unfathomable wisdom
find

to fulfill your truth and be merciful,
and to satisfy your justice as well?
What remedy did you give us?
O see what a fitting remedy!
You arranged to give us the Word, your only-
    begotten Son.
He would take of the clay of our flesh which had
    offended you
so that when he suffered in that humanity
your justice would be satisfied—
not by humanity's power,
but by the power of divinity united with that
    humanity.
And so, your truth was fulfilled,
and both justice and mercy were satisfied.

O Mary, I see this Word given to you, living in
    you
yet not separated from the Father—
just as the word one has in one's mind does not
    leave one's heart
or become separated from it
even though that word is externalized and
communicated to others.
In these things our human dignity is revealed—
that God should have done such and so great
    things for us.

And even more: in you, O Mary,
our human strength and freedom are today
        revealed,
for after the deliberation of such and so great a
        council,
the angel was sent to you to announce to you the
        mystery of the divine counsel
        and to seek to know your will,
and God's Son did not come down to your womb
until you had given your will's consent.
He waited at the door of your will for you to open
to him.
for he wanted to come into you, but he would
        never have entered
unless you had opened to him, saying,
"Here I am, God's servant; let it be done to me as
        you have said."

The strength and freedom of the will is clearly
        revealed, then,
for no good nor any evil can be done without that
        will.
Nor is there any devil or any other creature that
        can
drive it to the guilt of deadly sin without its
        consent.
Nor, on the other hand, can it be driven to do
        anything good

unless it so chooses.

So, the human will is free, for nothing can drive it
     to evil

or to good unless it so chooses.

The eternal Godhead, O Mary, was knocking at
     your door,

but unless you had opened that door of your will,

God would not have taken flesh in you.

Blush, my soul, when you see that

today God has become your relative in Mary.

Today you have been shown that even though

you were made without your help,

you will not be saved without your help.

For today God is knocking at the door of Mary's
     will and

waiting for her to open to Him.


O Mary, my tenderest love!

In you is written the Word from whom we have
     the teaching of life.

You are the tablet that sets this teaching before us.

I see that this Word, once written in you,

was never without the cross of holy desire.

Even as He was conceived within you,

desire to die for the salvation of humankind

was engrafted and bound into Him.

This is why He had been made flesh.

So, it was a great cross for Him to carry for such a

long time
that desire, when He would have liked to see it
    realized at once.
In fact, the Godhead was united even with Christ's
    body in the tomb
and with His soul in limbo,
and afterwards with both His soul and body.
The relationship was so entered into and sealed
that it will never be dissolved,
any more than it has been broken up to now. Amen.

*Saint Catherine of Siena*[7]

Saint John Eudes (c.1601–1680) is largely responsible for promulgating widespread devotion to the Sacred Heart of Jesus and the Immaculate Heart of Mary. Aware of a few mysteries of the Most Holy Trinity, he celebrated Christian feminism long before the word entered human consciousness. Founder of the Good Shepherd Nuns and the Society of Jesus and Mary (the Eudist Fathers), his motto was: "Love Jesus Christ with the immaculate heart of Mary and love Mary with the Sacred Heart of Jesus Christ." Pope Leo XIII declared him Father, Doctor and Apostle of the Sacred Heart of Jesus and the Immaculate Heart of Mary.

Hail Mary! Daughter of God the Father.

Hail Mary! Mother of God the Son.

Hail Mary! Spouse of the Holy Spirit.

Hail Mary! Temple of the Most Blessed Trinity.

Hail Mary! Pure Lily of the Effulgent Trinity.

Hail Mary! Celestial Rose of the ineffable Love of
God.

Hail Mary! Virgin pure and humble, of whom the
King of Heaven willed to be born and with
thy milk to be nourished.

Hail Mary! Virgin of Virgins,

Hail Mary! Queen of Martyrs, whose soul a sword
transfixed,

Hail Mary! Lady most blessed! unto whom all
power in heaven and earth is given.

Hail Mary! My Queen and my Mother! my Life,
my Sweetness and my Hope,

Hail Mary! Mother Most Amiable,

Hail Mary! Mother Most Admirable,

Hail Mary! Mother of Divine Love,

Hail Mary! Immaculate! Conceived Without
Sin!

Hail Mary! Full of Grace! The Lord is with
Thee!

Blessed art thou among women! And blessed is
the Fruit of thy womb, Jesus!

Blessed be thy spouse, Saint Joseph,

Blessed be thy father, Saint Joachim,

Blessed be thy mother, Saint Anne,

Blessed be thy protector, Saint John,
Blessed be thy holy angel, Saint Gabriel,
Glory be to God the Father, who chose thee,
Glory be to God the Son, who loves thee,
Glory be to God the Holy Spirit, who espoused
thee.

O Glorious Virgin Mary, may all people love and
praise thee.
Mary, Mother of God made flesh of thee! pray for
us and bless us now and at death in the Name of
Jesus, Thy Divine Son. Amen.

*Saint John Eudes*

Saint Bernardino of Siena (c. 1380–1444), descendant of Sienese
nobility, was a sacrificial and highly effective Franciscan missionary who discerned a scintilla of the mystery of Mary, the Most
Holy Mother of God. His parents died when he was seven years
old. This Saint survived the plague that ravaged Siena by turning
to Mary for his maternal consolations. Beginning in early childhood, he practiced continuous prayer, penance and fasting as a
preferred way of life for the glory of God. Bernardino experienced
Mary's tender spiritual nurturing, sacred wisdom and celestial care
that brought him into the depths of divine love within the Sacred
Heart of Jesus Christ. He shares this prayer.

O Mother Mary, holiest of women,
filled with blessings above all creatures,
You are the only Mother of God.
You are the Queen of the Universe.
You are the dispenser of all graces.
You are the ornament of the Church.
In you is contained the incomprehensible
    greatness of all virtue, and all gifts.
You are the temple of God,
the paradise of delight,
the model of all the just,
the consolation of your children,
the glory and source of our salvation.
You are the gate of heaven, the joy of the elect,
the object of God's great Plan for His holy people.
Though we only imperfectly celebrate your
    praises,
your love for us overcomes all our deficiencies.
May we worthily praise you, our Mother in God,
for all eternity. Amen.

*Saint Bernardino of Siena*

Saint Basil the Great (c. 329–379), highly esteemed Doctor of the Church, is the Patron Saint of Russia and the Patriarch of Eastern Monasticism. He was born into a family of saints, all of whom were devoted to Most Holy Mary, including his father, Saint Basil the Elder, his mother, Saint Emelia, his brother, Saint Gregory of Nyssa, his sister, Saint Macrina the Younger, and his grandmother, Saint Macrina. Though the family was affluent and influential by earthly standards, Basil responded heroically to a divine call to live in continuous prayer, penance and voluntary poverty. Young Basil led his family in understanding the place of created things in God's Plan for the human race. His principles and rules continue to guide monasteries of the Eastern Church.

O Holy Mary who are full of grace, all creation rejoices in you!
The hierarchies of the angels and the race of men rejoice.
O sanctified temple and rational paradise, virginal glory, of whom God took flesh!
He who is God before all ages, became a child.
Your womb He made His Throne,
and your lap He made greater than the heavens.
Indeed, all creation exults in you.
Glory be to you!

*From the Byzantine Liturgy of Saint Basil*

Saint Bonaventure (c. 1221–1274), beloved Doctor of the Church, was an Italian Franciscan who studied and taught Scripture and theology in Paris. A contemporary of Saint Thomas Aquinas, he is revered as one of the most influential medieval Church Fathers. His peers noted that he was a man of extraordinary prayer and asceticism for the glory of God. Humble and caring to sincere seekers, Saint Bonaventure was guided on his earthly path to the depths of the Sacred Heart of Christ by his divinely inspired love for Mother Mary. Bonaventure is known as the Seraphic Doctor of the Church. His many works illumine hints of our Heavenly Father's unfathomable, unconditional love and longing for His prodigal children of the earth.

O Mary, let me always remember when you
comprehended the depths of the love of the Eternal
Father toward the human race to be so great that,
in order to save them, He willed the death of His Son,
and on the other hand,
seeing the love of the Son in wishing to honor His
Father perfectly and therefore, to die for us:
in order to conform yourself, who was always and
 in all things united to the will of God,
to this excessive love of both the Father and the
Son towards the human race,

you also, with your entire will offered,
and consented to the death of your Son,
in order that we might be saved.

*Saint Bonaventure*

Saint Francis of Assisi (c. 1181–1226) is renowned throughout the world for many reasons. He embraced continuous prayer and voluntary poverty as he founded the Franciscan Order of Priests, Brothers, and Sisters. Saint Francis of Assisi heroically bore the wounds of Christ in his own body. He bequeathed future generations his joy-filled love for God, the Blessed Virgin Mary, the angels and saints, all people, animals and things God made. Divine Mercy allowed him to draw near God's tender, unconditional love and gentleness flowing from Holy Mother Mary through, with and in her fully human and fully divine Redeemer Infant son Jesus, the Christ who blesses and saves and restores all creation.

Hail, holy Lady, most holy Queen,
Mary, Mother of God, ever Virgin
Chosen by the most holy Father in heaven,
Consecrated by Him,
With His most holy, beloved Son
And the Holy Spirit, the Comforter.

On you descended, and in you still remains
All the fullness of grace and every good.
Hail, His Palace. Hail, His Tabernacle.
Hail, His Robe. Hail, His Handmaid.
Hail, His Mother. And hail, all holy virtues,
Who, by the grace and inspiration of the Holy Spirit,
Are poured into the hearts of the faithful
So that, faithless no longer, they may be made
Faithful children of God through you. Amen.

*Saint Francis of Assisi*

## THE MOTHER OF GOD

*The title Mother of God,*
*Theotokos, or God-bearer, was sanctioned at*
*the Council of Ephesus in 431.*

Hail to the Mother of God,
Hail to the Spouse of God Almighty,
Hail to the Flower of Grace Divine!
Hail to the heir of David's line!
Hail to the world's great Heroine!
Hail to the Virgin pre-elect!
Hail to the Work without defect
Of the Supernal Architect!
Hail to the Maid ordained of old,
Deep in eternities untold,

Ere the blue waves of ocean rolled!
Ere the perennial founts had sprung,
Ere in either the globe was hung,
Ere the morning stars had sung.
Welcome the beatific morn
When the Mother of Life was born—
Only hope of a world forlorn!
What a thrill of ecstatic mirth
Danced along through Heaven and Earth
At the tiding of Mary's birth!
Happy, happy the angel band
Chosen by Mary's side to stand,
As her defense on either hand!
Safe beneath our viewless wings,
Mother elect of the King of kings,
Fear no harm from hurtful things.
What though Eden vanished be,
More than Eden we find in thee!
Thou our joy and jubilee!

*Attributed to Rev. Edward Caswell (c. 1900)*

O Mother-Maiden! O Maid and Mother free!
O bush unburnt, burning in Moses' sight!
That down didst ravish from the Deity,
Through humbleness, the Spirit that did alight,
upon thy heart, whence, through that glory's might,

conceived was thy father's sapience!
Lady, thy goodness, thy magnificence,
Thy virtue, and thy great humility,
Surpass all science and all utterances.
For sometimes, Lady! ere men pray to thee,
Thou goest before in thy benignity,
The light to us vouchsafing to our prayer,
To be our guide unto thy Son so dear.

My knowledge is so weak, O blissful Queen,
To tell abroad thy mighty worthiness,
That I the weight of it may not sustain.
But as a child of twelve months old, or less,
That laboreth his language to express
Even so fare I; and therefore, I thee pray,
Guide thou my song, which I of thee shall say.

*Geoffrey Chaucer (c. 1342–1400)*
*Modernized by William Wordsworth*

Virgin and Mother of our dear Redeemer,
All hearts are touched and softened at your name.
Alike the bandit, with the blood-stained hand,
The priest, the prince, the scholar and the peasant,
The man of deeds, the visionary dreamer,
Pay homage to you as here always present.

And even as children, who have much offended
A too indulgent Father, in great shame,
Penitent, and yet not daring unattended
To go into His Presence, at the Gate
Speak with their Mother, and confiding wait
Till she goes in before and intercedes:
So, men, repenting of their evil deeds,
And yet not venturing rashly to draw near
With their requests a grieved Father's ear,
Offer to you their prayers and their confession,
And you for them in heaven make intercession.
And if our faith had given us nothing more,
Then this example of perfect Womanhood,
So mild, so merciful, so strong, so good,
So patient, so peaceful, loyal, loving, pure—
This were enough to prove it higher and truer than
All the creeds the world had ever known before.

*Henry Wadsworth Longfellow (c. 1807–1882)*

Ave Maria! o'er the earth and sea,
That heavenliest hour of heaven is worthiest thee!
Ave Maria! blessed be the hour
The time, the chime, the spot, where I so oft
Have felt that moment in its fullest power
Sink o'er the earth so beautiful and soft

While swung the deep bell in the distant tower,
Or the faint dying day hymn stole aloft,
And not a breath crept through the rosy air,
And yet the forest leaves seemed stirred with prayer.

Ave Maria! 'tis the hour of prayer.
Ave Maria! 'tis the hour of love.
Ave Maria! may our spirits dare
Look up to thine and to thy Son's above.
Ave Maria! oh, that face so fair,
Those downcast eyes beneath the Almighty Dove!

*Lord George Noel Gordon Byron (c. 1788–1824)*

The wandering shepherds told their breathless tale
Of the bright choir that woke the sleeping vale.
Told how the shining multitude proclaimed.
They spoke with hurried words and accents wild.
Calm in His cradle slept the heavenly Child.
No trembling word your Motherly joy revealed, —
One sigh of rapture, and your lips were sealed.

*Oliver Wendell Holmes (c. 1809–1894)*

## CHAPTER 3

# MOTHER MOST POWERFUL

*Prayers of Consecration*

Through the centuries, humble, godly people have conse-crated their hearts, families, yesterdays and tomorrows to Jesus Christ through His Holy Mother Mary. In so doing, dedicated believers trust that our Heavenly Mother Mary will tenderly and most perfectly present everyone and everything to her Son with love beyond telling. Saint John Paul II travelled the world teaching his faith-filled understanding of All-Holy Mother Mary, Our Lady of Cana as undefiled intercessor of all God's beloved people.[1]

By consecration to Christ through Mary, we enter into a reciprocal heavenly entrustment steeped in faith, hope and love as we convey ourselves and all the longings of our hearts, minds and souls into the safe-keeping of our Heavenly Mother Mary for her Son Jesus the Christ. This entrustment appoints Mary as guardian and keeper of all that matters to us so that nothing we love is ever lost. By this type of prayerful consecration, we place ourselves and everything we hold dear into Mother Mary's heavenly custody for Jesus Christ. Mother Mary knows her Son well. Purest maiden of humankind, Mary knows what Christ likes and how He likes to receive, renew and glorify everything for our Heavenly Father.

Saint Bernard of Clairvaux (c.1090–1153) had the privilege of personal mentoring by our Heavenly Mother Mary. Consider the directive of this great French Doctor of the Church regarding all gifts to Christ through Mary, especially the gift of ourselves.

"If you wish to offer anything to God, do not forget to present it through Mary, in order that Grace may return to its Author through the same channel by which it came to you; for God, no doubt could have bestowed His graces without her mediation, but He wished to provide you with a pure means of returning to Him. Perhaps your hands are stained with blood or soiled by things you should have rejected. Therefore, it is that the little you desire to offer should be presented by the pure and worthy hands of Mary. You may then be secure that your offering will not be despised. Her hands are like the pure and spotless lily, and He who loves the lily will be pleased to see among the lilies the modest gift which you present to Him through the hands of Mary."

Six hundred years later, Saint Louis de Montfort bequeathed us his directives concerning consecration to our Heavenly Mother Mary:

"All our perfection consists in being conformed, united, and consecrated to Jesus Christ: and therefore, the most perfect of all devotions is, without any doubt, that which perfectly conforms, unites and consecrates us to Christ. Now, Mary being the most conformed of all creatures to Jesus Christ, that which most consecrates and conforms the soul to Our Lord is devotion to His Holy Mother, and the more a soul is consecrated to Mary, the more it is consecrated to Jesus Christ. Hence it comes to pass that the most perfect consecration to Jesus Christ is nothing less than a perfect and entire consecration of ourselves to the Blessed Virgin, and this is the devotion I teach; a perfect renewal of the vows and promises of Baptism.

"This devotion consists in giving ourselves entirely to Mary in order to belong entirely to Jesus Christ through her. We must give her:

1. our body, with all its senses and members
2. our soul, with all its powers

3.  our exterior goods of fortune, whether present or to come
4.  our interior and spiritual goods, which are our merits and our virtues, and our good works, past, present and future. . .

"We give to her all our merits, graces and virtues—not to communicate them to others, for our merits, graces and virtues are, properly speaking, incommunicable, and it is only Jesus Christ Who, in making Himself our surety with His Father, is able to communicate His merits—but we give them to her to keep them, augment them and embellish them for us.

"Our satisfactions, however, we give her, to communicate to whom she likes, and for the greatest glory of God . . . By this devotion, we give to Jesus Christ in the most perfect manner, by Mary's hands, all we can give to Him . . . Here, everything is given and consecrated to Him, even the right of disposing of our interior goods, and of the satisfactions which we gain by our good works day after day . . .

"We consecrate ourselves at one and the same time to the most Holy Virgin and to Jesus Christ: to the most Holy Virgin as to the perfect means which Jesus Christ has chosen whereby to unite Himself to us, and us to Him; and to Our Lord as to our last end, to Whom as our Redeemer and our God we owe all."

The value of family consecrations was reinforced for an American family in an unusual way. Before their children were born, a Christian couple consecrated each of their yet to be born children to the Immaculate Heart of Mary for the Sacred Heart of Jesus, in accordance with their faith tradition. As their children grew into adulthood, the family decided to increase their level of commitment to their faith beliefs. After the youngest child finished high school, the entire family journeyed to a Marian Shrine far from home. Each one personally prayed and fasted in preparation for the trip and joined in daily family prayer.

At dawn on the first morning of the pilgrimage to the Shrine, the parents climbed a tall mountain and knelt before a huge cross in quiet prayer. There, praying together, they reconsecrated their nearly-grown children to the Immaculate Heart of Mary for her Son Jesus Christ. No one was nearby. Several hours later, a young villager whom they did not know at the time, approached the family. The villager said to the parents: "The Blessed Mother asked me to thank you for giving your children back to her. She said they are better off with her."

Only in deepest faith and trust are we able to hand over to Mary what we hold most dear. Yet God had such great faith in her, and so unreservedly trusted her, that He became Mary's helpless Infant, allowing Himself to be totally dependent on her for every human need. If God so entrusts Himself to Mary, why shouldn't we?

A famous nun from long ago, Saint Gertrude the Great (c. 1256–c. 1302), lives on powerfully in our collective memory. Mary appeared to the German Benedictine Sister with the following promise that is as valid today as it was in Saint Gertrude's lifetime:

> "I will appear at the hour of death to those who pray to me as the *White Lily of the Ever Peaceful and Glorious Trinity* with such glory that they will experience the very joys of Heaven."

In response, the saint composed this prayer of consecration that binds us to our Heavenly Mother Mary's great promise.

### PRAYER OF SAINT GERTRUDE THE GREAT

Hail Mary, White Lily of the ever peaceful and
glorious Trinity!
Hail Vermilion Rose, the Delight of Heaven,
Of whom, the King of Heaven was born,
And by whose milk He was nourished!
Do thou forever feed our souls by the effusions of
your divine influences.
Amen.

*Saint Gertrude the Great*

On the Polish mountain of Jasna Gora that overlooks the city of Czestochowa stands the famous Shrine of Our Lady of Czestochowa, considered by many to be one of the holiest places on earth. Contained in the Shrine is the ancient and greatly venerated image of the "Black Madonna."

Pope Saint John Paul II led the world in consecration to Christ through Mary as he knelt before the holy image of the Black Madonna. The Consecration Prayer to Our Lady of Czestochowa the Pope prayed at Jasna Gora is recommended daily upon arising.

Holy Mother of Czestochowa, you are full of
 grace, goodness and mercy.
I consecrate to you all my thoughts, words and
 actions, my soul and body.
I beseech your blessings and especially prayers
For my salvation.
Today I consecrate myself to you, Good Mother,
totally with body and soul amid joy and sufferings
to obtain for myself and others your blessings on
this earth and eternal life in heaven. Amen.

Few men of such worldwide eminence publicly extoled the virtues and glories of the Blessed Virgin Mary as eloquently as Pope Saint John Paul II. He, having overcome an assassin's bullet, entrusted world peace to our Heavenly Mother Mary. Fearlessly, Saint John Paul II encouraged others to do likewise. The following is a personal consecration to Jesus Christ through All-Holy Mother Mary that he prayed daily.

In the presence of all the heavenly court I choose thee this day for my Mother and mistress. I deliver and consecrate to thee, as thy slave, my body and soul, my goods, both interior and exterior, and even the value of all my good actions, past, present and future; leaving to thee the entire and full right of disposing of me, and all that belongs to me without exception, according to thy good pleasure, for the greater glory of God in time and eternity.

*Saint Louis Marie Grignon de Montfort, (c. 1713)*

## MORNING PRAYER OF ATONEMENT

O Jesus, through the Immaculate Heart of Mary, and in union with the Holy Sacrifice of the Mass

being offered throughout the world, I offer You
all my prayers, works, joys and sufferings of this
day in atonement for offenses committed against
Your Sovereignty, against the Immaculate Heart
of Mary, for my sins and the sins of the whole
world. Amen.

*Author Unknown*

For those who may not have known about the consecration life
offering until now, various versions of the following prayer, taught
in Catholic schools for generations, may be helpful.

### LIFE CONSECRATION PRAYER

O my God, in union with the Lord Jesus Christ,
through the Immaculate Heart of Mary,
I offer to you my entire life, just as it is,
from the moment You breathed me out of Your
Infinite Heart of Love into my mother's womb,
until that moment when my life on earth is
spent. I offer to You all my handicaps and weaknesses, past mistakes and failures, talents and
abilities, all the joys, sorrows, blessings, disappointments and victories of my entire life.

I entrust to Your mercy my past and my future.
I place in Your Hands my family and loved ones:
those who are living now on earth, those who
 preceded me and those yet to be born. I offer
to You all that happens to me this day and every
day of my life, together with all my thoughts,
words and deeds, for Your great honor and glory
and for the salvation of souls. May Your perfect
Plan be realized in my life. Amen.

*Anonymous*

## FÁTIMA PRAYER OF CONSECRATION

O Virgin of Fátima, Mother of Mercy, Queen of
    Heaven and earth, Refuge of Sinners, we conse-
crate ourselves to your Immaculate Heart
in order to enter into a more intimate relationship
with your Divine Son, Jesus Christ.
To you we consecrate our hearts, our families and
    all that we have.
So that this consecration may be effective and last-
ing, we renew today, and every day, the promises of
    our Baptism:
we promise to live as faithful Christians, to read
    the sacred scriptures,
to pray, especially the Holy Rosary, to

partake of the Holy Eucharist, to observe the
First Saturdays of Atonement each month,
and to work and sacrifice for the conversion of
sinners, especially ourselves.
We pray that through your intercession
the coming of the Kingdom of Christ may be
hastened. Amen.

*National Shrine of Our Lady of Fatima*

## DAILY OFFERING PRAYER

O Jesus, through the Immaculate Heart of Mary,
I offer You all my prayers, works, joys and
sufferings,
all that this day may bring,
be they good or bad:
for the love of God,
for the conversion of sinners,
and in atonement for all the sins committed
against the Sacred Heart of Jesus and
the Immaculate Heart of Mary. Amen.

*Anonymous*

## THREE SACRED PRAYERS OF
## CONSECRATION TO MARY

Most Holy Virgin, I venerate you with my whole
    heart,
above all the angels and saints in Paradise,
as the Daughter of the Eternal Father,
and I consecrate to you my soul with all its
    powers.
(*Pray the Hail Mary.*)

Most Holy Virgin, I venerate you with my whole
    heart,
above all the angels and saints in Paradise,
as the Mother of the only begotten Son,
and I consecrate to you my body with all its
    senses.
(*Pray the Hail Mary.*)

Most Holy Virgin, I venerate you with my whole
    heart,
above all the angels and saints in Paradise,
as the Spouse of the Holy Spirit,
and I consecrate to you my whole heart and all its
    affections,
praying you to obtain for me,
from the ever-blessed Trinity,
all that is necessary for my salvation.
(*Pray the Hail Mary.*)

*Author Unknown*

The following prayer is a special Consecration Prayer to Our Lady of Guadalupe, the title that signifies Mary apparitions to Saint Juan Diego in Mexico City in 1531.

O Most Holy Virgin Mary, Mother of God,
I (*mention name*), although most unworthy of
 being your servant,
Yet touched by your wonderful mercy and by the
 desire to serve,
consecrate myself to your Immaculate Heart, and
 choose you today,
in the presence of my Guardian Angel and the
 whole heavenly court, for my special Mother,
 Lady, and Advocate, under the title of
Our Lady of Guadalupe, the name given to the
 heavenly image,
left to us as a pledge of your motherly kindness.
I firmly resolve that I will love and serve you
 always,
and do whatever I can to induce others to love and
 serve you.
I pray to you Mother of God, and my most kind
 and amiable Mother,
that you receive me into your family,
and keep me as your special child forever.
Assist me in all thoughts, words and actions at
 every moment of my life,

that every step and breath may be directed to the
    greater glory of God.
And through your most powerful intercession,
    obtain for me that
I may never more offend my Lord Jesus, that I
    may glorify Him
in this life, and that I may also love you, and be
    with you,
in the company of the Blessed Trinity throughout
    eternity in holy Paradise.
In order to live this consecration as did Saint Juan Diego,
I promise to renew it frequently,
especially on the twelfth day of each month.
And mindful of your messages to us at Lourdes and
Fatima,
I will strive to lead a life of prayer and sacrifice, of
    fidelity to the Holy Rosary
and of atonement through your Immaculate Heart.
    Amen.[2]

Jesuit John Carroll was the first Archbishop of the United States. His family risked everything in 1776 when his brother Daniel Carroll signed the Declaration of Independence. In 1792, Archbishop John Carroll publicly implored the Lord God to forever safeguard the young nation under the gracious, maternal protection of Mary in his solemn consecration that follows.

## CONSECRATION PRAYER OF THE UNITED STATES TO MARY

Most Holy Trinity, Our Father in Heaven,
Who chose Mary as the fairest of Your daughters,
Holy Spirit Who chose Mary as Your Spouse,
God the Son Who chose Mary as Your Mother,
In union with Mary, we adore Your Majesty
And acknowledge Your supreme, eternal dominion
    and authority.

Most Holy Trinity, we place the United States of
    America
Into the hands of Mary Immaculate
In order that she may present the country
To You.
Through her we wish to thank You for the great
    resources of this land
And for the freedom which has been its heritage.

Through the intercession of Mary, have mercy on
    the catholic church in America.
Grant us peace.
Have mercy on our President
And on all the officers of our government.

Grant us a fruitful economy, born of justice and
    labor.
Protect the family life of the nation.
Guard the precious gift of many religious vocations.
Through the intercession of Mary Our Mother,
    have mercy on the sick,
The tempted, sinners . . . on all who are in need.

Mary, Immaculate Virgin, Our Mother,
Patroness of our land, we praise and honor you
And give ourselves to you.
Protect us from every harm.
Pray for us, that acting always according to your
    will
And the will of your Divine Son,
We may live and die pleasing to God. Amen.[3]

*Archbishop John Carroll*

## CONSECRATION PRAYER
## FOR THE UNITED STATES

God our Father, Giver of life,
we entrust the United States of America to
Your loving care.
You are the rock on which this nation was
    founded.

You alone are the true source of
our cherished rights to life, liberty
and the pursuit of happiness.
Reclaim this land for Your glory
and dwell among Your people.

Send Your Spirit to touch the hearts of
our nation's leaders.
Open their minds to the great worth
of human life and the responsibilities
that accompany human freedom.
Remind Your people that true happiness
is rooted in seeking and doing Your will.

Through the intercession of Mary
Immaculate, Patroness of our land,
grant us the courage to reject
the "culture of death."
Lead us into a new millennium of life.
We ask this through Christ our Lord. Amen.[4]

CONSECRATION PRAYER FOR CREATION

O divine eternal unchanging Creator
How great is Thy love.
How great is Thy creation.

How great is Thy Mercy.
O True God, Thou alone are Perfection.
O True God, Thou alone need nothing.
Yet, in Thine infinite perfection,
Alone, Thee allow every prayer we pray
To draw upon each of us and Thy creation
The healing measures of Thine infinite perfection.
O divine eternal unchanging Creator,
Thou hast freely willed to need us.
In Mary, Mother Maiden Most Pure,
Thy Word embraced us in mystery
And dwelt among us creatures,
Thy prodigal children of earth.
To Thee and to Thy great Plan
 O Great Mystery of the Incarnation,
We poor creatures surrender.
And we consecrate ourselves, our families,
Possessions, earth and sun and seas
And stars and sands and skies and streams.
Image and likeness of Thee are we
Who freely present all these to Thee
Of Mary, Your Mother Maiden Most Pure
Who dwells in Thee Who rules all these.
Infinite Babe of Thy Mother Maiden Most Pure,
From Mary's heart alone flows earth pure to Thee
To please, Your Mother Maiden Most Pure,
Forever earth pure
Of Thee, Mary's Babe, divine, eternal,

Source of creation, Heaven pure.
Sing and dance and pray upon creation pure
For the old has passed away
In the Immaculate Heart of earth pure,
Mary, God's Mother Maiden Most Pure.
In her dwells Earth and Heaven pure,
Mary's Babe, divine, eternal,
Source of creation, Jesus the Christ,
Lord of lords, forever.  Amen.

*Anonymous*

## CHAPTER 4

# MOTHER MOST AMIABLE

*Prayers for Groups*

The Lord Jesus Christ promised that wherever two or more are gathered in His name, He is present.[1] That is one of His calls to form prayer groups. Prayer groups can be as simple or as elaborate as participants' desire.

A prayer group can be formed anywhere by a single person and his or her guardian angel. It can also be a husband and wife, parent and child, two co-workers, or even two children on a playground who pause and pray together. A prayer group can include hundreds of thousands of people who gather in fields and stadiums to pray. A prayer group can meet in a place of worship or under the stars. There may be a prayer leader, perhaps a priest, minister, rabbi, sister, or a lay member selected by the group. When there is no specific leader, participants may prefer to take turns reading prayers or scripture passages aloud. Some prayer groups like to join hands around their family dinner table. Regardless of the size or approach, prayer groups strengthen participants' faith, trust in God, and ability to make more loving choices.

## MARY'S PRAYER GROUPS

Marian prayer groups have a long history. The good thief crucified beside Jesus on Golgotha perhaps glimpsed Mother Mary and her tiny prayer group abiding with crucified Jesus. Did he experience Mary's tender and compassionate love for him as she consoled her dying Son? Involuntarily, two thieves were included in Mary's prayer group at Calvary. One thief, now known as Saint Dismas, reached out to Jesus. No one really knows why. Those who emulate the Good Thief trust Jesus shall fulfill His promise: "*Today you will be with me in Paradise*"[2].

Since that Marian prayer group at Calvary, groups have continued to praise, honor and console Christ with and through Mary. Historically, Marian groups aspire to total loyalty to Christ in good times and bad. Their duty is to live their faith to the best of their ability and transmit it to subsequent generations.

A paradox of Christ through Mary: whatever honors, praise or graciousness we extend to Mary are Christ's love for her flowing through us responding to His grace. This is a most powerful spiritual force.

Fervent souls are inevitably drawn to Mary in a special way. All little brothers and sisters of Jesus for whom He died on Calvary are drawn by His grace to extend imperfect manifestations of

· Christ's filial love for His Mother. In all times, places and ways, in every expression of love for Mary, it is always Christ who honors and loves His Mother through children of Mary on earth and in Heaven

Contemporary Knights and Dames of the thousand-year-old world-wide Order of Malta honor Christ through Mary under her title "Our Lady of Palermo." In the United States, there are approximately 140,000 members of the Catholic Daughters of America who profess a special devotion to Christ through Mary. Knights of Columbus are renowned as filial sons of Mary for Christ. Many shrines in the United States and throughout the world, such as the National Blue Army Shrine of Our Lady of Fatima, to name only one, have strong traditions of honoring Christ through Mary. More than five hundred years ago, a Jesuit Doctor of the Church, Saint Peter Canisius, was instrumental in founding the Sodality of Our Lady to enlist people to work for the Kingdom of God throughout the world. Sodalists are known as children of Mary.

The Legion of Mary is another Marian prayer group with a global presence. Like other Marian groups, the Legion of Mary requires its members to pray together and serve the less fortunate. Magnificat Ministries was formed in New Orleans at the end of the last century and includes chapters globally. Countless informal Rosary prayer groups have sprung up among students, parents, grandparents, families, leaders, employers and employees, neighbors and friends throughout the world.

Marian prayer groups effectively call for members to imitate Mother Mary and Apostle John who fearlessly stood by Jesus

Christ at Golgotha. The humble goal of all Marian organizations is total loyalty to Christ through Mary.

Many Marian prayer groups are a spontaneous grassroots effort of people all over the earth seeking to meet the deepest needs of their hearts. Often people join or form Marian prayer groups as protection against the evil being unmasked everywhere. In these technological times, there are few places, if any, to hide.

One of the benefits of belonging to a Marian prayer group is the confidence God instills in members through Mother Mary that the Lord will bring a successful conclusion to human endeavors as long as each person does his or her utmost in prayer, work and service to the less fortunate.[3] With sincere personal prayer, generous almsgiving and fasting discipline, people are capable of consciously focusing on the divine love and providence of God around us, in us and always with us. That focus ripens into awareness of the reciprocal love relationship flowing between God and His prodigal children.[4]

Marian prayer groups usually begin by invoking the promised presence of the Lord Jesus Christ among them. Mary, the angels and saints are then invited to join with the group in prayer and praise. Amazing experiences are reported all over the world by those who pray, praise, study Scripture and sing together in this way.

Marian prayer group members aim to help one another faithfully follow Christ and imitate His life of prayer, praise, sacrificial acts of kindness, mercy and penance for the glory of our Heavenly Father. In many diverse ways, participants aspire to pray, meditate, fast, embrace penance and almsgiving as a way of life. No particular way is best. Members are encouraged to consciously discipline themselves by eliminating time consuming, frivolous pleasures in imitation of Christ.

Personal sentiments, like the tides of the ocean, change and come and go. We all belong to a particular reality outside of ourselves and yet deep within us. Authentic fruits of Marian prayer groups are shared joy and tranquility among diverse members. Moderation, in harmony with God, nature and neighbor spawns a life of simplicity and balance that is an underlying goal of all Marian prayer groups. Heightened awareness of Divine Providence, nature, and neighborly needs, coupled with joyful almsgiving, are outflows of Marian prayer groups.

Eminent Marian theologian René Laurentin identified some guidelines for Mary's prayer groups. Several of the more practiced ones choose to follow them, perhaps because they bring form, meaning, and order to the vicissitudes of life minute by minute. Those just beginning or joining an on-going Marian prayer group follow as many as are suitable in their circumstances. Gradually, the wisdom of the guidelines becomes evident and with perseverance, they become a source of Light.

1. Renounce all inordinate passions and desires. Pray for discernment. Practice acknowledging God's loving, providential omnipresence with faith and gratitude.
2. Be spiritually circumspect in the use of cyberspace.
3. Abandon yourselves to God without any restrictions.

4.  Eliminate anguish and worry. Whoever abandons himself to God has no place in his heart for negativity. Difficulties will persist, but they serve for spiritual growth and bring great glory to God.

5.  Love your enemies. Banish bitterness, hatred, prejudice, preconceived judgments. Pray for your enemies and call the divine blessing over them.

6.  Fast twice a week as a love offering to God.

7.  Extend the spirit of prayer to all daily work and activities. Devote at least three hours each day to conscious prayer, meditation and service to others for the glory of God. Reserve a half hour or more at the beginning and conclusion of each day for deep intimacy with the Lord. When possible, include daily participation in Holy Mass with reception of the Holy Eucharist. Pray the Holy Rosary every day with great love, meditation, concentration and awareness. Set aside times during the day to mentally adore and console Jesus Christ truly present in the Most Blessed Sacrament in tabernacles throughout the world. If your faith in the Real Presence of Christ in the Eucharist is weak or nonexistent, ask the angels to do it for you until your faith expands. Allow yourselves to be led by the grace of God. Do not focus upon the problems of the day; give them to Christ. The Lord brings solutions to

problems if each one strives to do his utmost in working, praying, obeying the Commandments and living the Beatitudes, not for self, but for the glory of God.

8. Be prudent. Pray for the virtue of prudence. Develop discernment. The evil one will tempt and taunt those who resolve to consecrate themselves to God. Only as faith is strengthened through prayer, fasting, penance and almsgiving is the power of the evil one diminished.

9. Pray fervently for the leadership in your home country and in the world. Offer prayers and sacrifices for them. [5]

Mary's prayer groups are for everyone. Each prayer helps melt cold, hardened human hearts. The blessings flowing out of each Marian prayer group draw down joy and happiness somewhere on the earth.

## GROUP PRAYER FOR FAITH

How can I praise you duly, O most chaste Virgin?
For you alone among humans are all holy, and you
give to all the help and grace they need.
All we who are on the earth put our hope in you:

strengthen our faith, shine through the dimness of
    this world,
while we, God's people, sing your praise.
Throne of the Cherubim are you
and Gate of Heaven.
Pray without ceasing for us
that we may be saved in the day of dread.
Amen.

*From the Liturgy of the Antiochene Syriac Rite*

## GROUP PRAYER FOR HELP

Let your intercession be with us, O Mother Most
Pure,
and come to us in our needs, as is your wont.
We are exiles on this earth, without end ever before
    our eyes, and even now many of us perish.
Help us by your prayers, O Merciful Mother.
Be always our advocate lest we are lost through
    our own ill will.
Blessed and most holy one, plead for us before God
that He may be gracious to us through your
    asking. Amen.

*From the Liturgy of the Maronite Rite*

## GROUP PRAYER FOR DELIVERANCE
## FROM DISTURBING TEMPTATIONS

O Mother of God, trusting in you we shall not be
    ashamed but saved.
Strengthened by your help and intercession,
O holy, pure and perfect one,
we shall resist our temptations and scatter them.
We take up the shelter of your aid as a strong
    shield,
and we supplicate you, O Mother of God,
that you preserve each of us through your prayers.
Lead us out of the darkness of sin to glorify the
    Almighty God Who took flesh in you. Amen.

*From the Liturgy of the*
*Coptic Office of Sleep, Alexandrian Rite*

## GROUP PRAYER FOR PROTECTION

We, faithful, hold a joyful feast today, shadowed
    by your coming.
O Mother of God,
praising and looking upon your most holy image,
we reverently say:
cover us with your sacred veil
and liberate us from all evil,

beseeching your Son, Christ our God,
to save our souls.
Amen.

*From the Liturgy of the Protection of the*
*Blessed Virgin, October 1*

The following is a popular consecration for family prayer groups.

### FAMILY CONSECRATION
### TO THE LORD JESUS CHRIST

ALL: Most kind Jesus, You alone are our Lord
and Ruler. Humbly kneeling before You, we
consecrate our family, living, deceased, and yet to
be born, to You forever. In You we have total trust
and confidence. May Your Spirit penetrate our
thoughts, desires, words and actions. Bless all our
undertakings, share in all our joys, our trials and all
our daily labors. Grant us to know You better, to
love You more, and to serve You faithfully without
faltering.

Lord Jesus Christ, Son of the Living God,
protect our family now and forever. Enter closely
into our midst and make each of us Your own

through this solemn consecration to You. By the Immaculate Heart of Your Blessed Mother, under her title "Queen of Peace," set up your kingdom of peace, love, and joy throughout the world. Grant that one cry may resound from every home on earth:

"May the Lord Jesus Christ be everywhere loved, blessed, and glorified now and forever."

(*Silence for meditation*)

He promised: "Whoever loves me will be loved by my Father, and I will love him and reveal myself to him.[6]

ALL: Come to us Lord Jesus Christ, come to us Lord Jesus Christ. Come to us Lord Jesus Christ. Amen.

*Anonymous*

The following prayer for conversion has been prayed successfully by groups in Europe and now comes to prayer groups in the United States. This prayer is also effective when prayed by one person and can be directed toward anyone for whom conversion is desired.

## GROUP PRAYER FOR THE
## CONVERSION OF A LOVED ONE

Your prayer group of sweet loving where I gave
    myself to you dear Mother Mary
Has filled me with a wonder that is full of
    thoughts of you.
My life is now poured out in love and work and
    prayer,
And yet, there is a sadness, for I long to help and
    speak of my thoughts of you.
The one whom Heaven gave me to share this life
    on earth
Has not yet received your gentle kiss and does not
    know your worth.
I long to share my happiness, the meaning of all
    your words,
To plan our lives around them and bring others to
    the Lord.
But "my love" views me with sorrow at all the time
    I take
In pondering your messages and praying for your
    sake.
O gentle Mother, hear me, please touch "my love"
    for me
That together we may journey with your Blessed
    Son and thee.

Let our family be a haven for the lonely and the weak
That we may bring your blessings when a
    messenger you seek.
May our home be full of laughter and abundance,
may our journey be a prayer.
Let our lives reflect the beauty of your loving and
    your care. Amen.

*Ishbel McGillivray-McGregor*

## FOR HEALING OF BODY, MIND, SPIRIT, RELATIONSHIPS

A prayer group format in honor of our Blessed Mother as Queen of Peace, which lends itself easily to a formal place of worship, was circulated throughout the world beginning in 1988. Ideally, this prayer service is conducted in front of the Blessed Sacrament.

The *Apostles' Creed*, the *Our Father, Hail Mary*, and *Glory Be to the Father* prayers, along with the Joyful, Luminous, Sorrowful, and Glorious Mysteries of the Holy Rosary, can be found in Chapter 9 of this book. In addition, the *Litany of Loreto* can be found in Chapter 7, and the *Magnificat* in Chapter 5.

ALL: We adore You, O most holy Lord Jesus Christ
and we bless You here and, in all places, where two

or more are gathered in Your Holy Name through-out the world.

ALL: Blessed be the Holy Trinity, one God, now and forever. Amen.

Glory to our Father, Who created me; glory to the Son, Who redeemed me; glory to the Holy Spirit, Who sanctifies me.

ALL: **Consecration to the Sacred Heart of Jesus**: Jesus, we know that You are merciful and that You have offered Your Heart for us. It is crowned with thorns and with our sins. We know that You implore us constantly so that we do not go astray. Jesus, remember us when we are in sin. By means of Your Heart, make all people love one another. Make hate disappear from among Your people. Show us Your love. We all love You and want You to protect us with Your Shepherd's Heart and free us from every sin. Jesus, enter into every heart. Knock! Knock at the door of our hearts. Be patient and never desist. We are still closed because we have not understood Your love. Knock continuously. O Good Jesus, make us open our hearts to You, at least in the moment we remem-ber Your Passion suffered for us. Amen.

ALL: **Consecration to the Immaculate Heart of Mary**: O Immaculate Heart of Mary, ardent with goodness, show your love to us. May the flame of your heart, O Mary, descend on all mankind. We love you so. Impress true love in our hearts so that we have a continuous desire for you. O Mary, meek and humble of heart, remember us when we are in sin. You know that all people sin. Give us, by means of your Immaculate Heart, spiritual health. Let us always see the goodness of your maternal heart, and may we be converted by means of the flames of God's love for us in your heart. Amen.

Jesus said: "Peace be with you . . . As the Father has sent me, so I send you".[7]

ALL: Lord Jesus, fill me with Your Holy Spirit that I may live Your Word and thereby be an instrument of Your peace to the ends of the earth.

Jesus said: "Be like servants who await their master's return.... You must be prepared, for at an hour you do not expect, the Son of Man will come".[8]

LEADER: Selected reading from Sacred Scripture

(*Short silence for meditation*)

ALL: Pray the Joyful Mysteries of the Holy Rosary. Pray the Luminous Mysteries of the Holy Rosary. Pray the Sorrowful Mysteries of the Holy Rosary. Pray the Glorious Mysteries of the Holy Rosary. Pray the Litany of Loreto. Pray the Magnificat.

(*In silence*)

O my God, I am heartily sorry for having offended You, and I detest all my sins because I dread the loss of Heaven and the pains of hell. But, most of all my God, because You are all good and deserving of all my love. I firmly resolve with the help of Your grace to confess my sins, do penance and amend my life. Amen.

(*Priest*) Holy Sacrifice of the Mass (with Homily)

ALL: **Prayer of Saint Michael the Archangel**

Saint Michael the Archangel defend us in battle: be our safeguard against the wickedness and snares of the devil. May God rebuke him, we humbly pray; and do you, Prince of the Heavenly Host, by the power of God, cast into hell all the evil spirits who wander through the world seeking the ruin of souls. Amen.

Apostles' Creed (*Priest leads*)

Pray seven Our Fathers, seven Hail Marys, seven Glory Be to the Fathers

Spontaneous Prayer and Blessing (*Priest*)

Everyone is invited share fellowship after the service.
*NOTE: The suggested format above may be, and frequently is, customized to fit time constraints, needs and location of each prayer group.*

## CHAPTER 5

# MOTHER OF OUR CREATOR

*Prayers for Holiness*

Each person on earth is created to be holy.[1] We hunger and thirst (consciously or unconsciously) for holiness, a synonym for perfect happiness.[2] The Lord Jesus commanded us to be perfect as our Heavenly Father is perfect.[3] Because God alone is perfectly holy, we continuously strive toward the perfection of holiness in our relentless pursuit of happiness.[4] Jesus Christ, truly God and truly man is the celestially radiant way, truth, and light for success in our quest for holiness—perfect happiness.[5]

Supernatural wisdom oversees our quest. The Holy Spirit, Mary's Spouse, is the source of supernatural wisdom by which we experience God's unconditional, pure love for us now.[6] The prayers in this chapter gently lead us along the luminous path of this sublime, supernatural gift.

Humility, flowing from supernatural wisdom, empowers us to seek perfect holiness.[7] A humble heart is open to God, and the humbler the heart, the more it is capable of knowing God who is pure love.[8] Humility is a condition of the soul.[9] Like the scent of a flower, it is known by its effects.[10] Many of the prayers in this chapter strengthen our deep, largely unconscious need to believe in and accept God's unfathomable love for us .[11]

Saint Mechtildis (c. 1241-1298) is a beloved Benedictine apostle of God's tender love and mercy who mentored Saint Gertrude the Great. The Lord endowed Mechtildis with a signal grace to help us consciously appreciate the value, joy and peace of holiness. Her wonder-filled revelations of the One True God are contained in her ***Book of Special Grace***. Even the great poet Dante, in his prophetic publication ***The Divine Comedy,*** was influenced by the supernatural wisdom imparted to Saint Mechtildis. As our colleague in prayer, Saint Mechtildis swiftly leads us to the immaculate heart of Mary so that our path to the Sacred Heart of Christ is made clearer and easier.

Saint Louis de Montfort, whom some consider a protégée of Saint Mechtildis, wrote a small spiritual masterpiece, ***True Devotion to Mary,*** that provides insights into the mysterious, wonderful blessings available to children of Mary.

"Oh, what a difference between a soul which has been formed in Christ by the ordinary ways of those who, like the sculptor, trust in their own skill and ingenuity, and a soul thoroughly tractable, entirely detached and well molten, which, without trusting to its own skill, casts itself into Mary, there to be molded by the Holy Spirit! How many stains and defects and illusions, how much darkness and how much human nature is there in the former, and oh, how pure, how heavenly and how Christlike is the latter!"

### PRAYER FOR THE SPIRIT OF MARY

My powerful Queen Mother,
you are all mine through your mercy,
and I am all yours.
Take away from me all that may displease God
and cultivate in me all that is pleasing to Him.

May the light of your faith
dispel the darkness of my mind,
your deep humility
take the place of my pride,
your continual sight of God
fill my memory with His Presence.

May the fire of the charity of your heart
inflame the luke warmness of my own heart.

May your virtues take the place of my sins.
May your merits be my enrichment
and make up for all
that is wanting in me before God.

My beloved Mother,
grant that I may have no other spirit but your spirit, to
know Jesus Christ and His Divine will
and to praise and glorify the Lord,
that I may love God with burning love like yours. [12]

*Saint Louis de Montfort, (c.1673-1716)*

Hail Mary, daughter of God the Father!
Hail Mary, Mother of God the Son!
Hail Mary, Spouse of the Holy Spirit!
Hail Mary, temple of the most Holy Trinity!
Hail Mary, my mistress, my wealth, my mystic rose,
Queen of my heart, my Mother, my life, my
    sweetness and my dearest hope.
I am all yours, and all that I have is yours, O Virgin
    blessed above all things.
May your soul be in me to magnify the Lord.
May your spirit be in me to rejoice in God.
Place yourself, O faithful Virgin, as a seal upon my
    heart that in you and through you, I may be found
    faithful to God.

Grant, most gracious Virgin, that I may be
numbered among those whom you are pleased to
love, to teach and to guide, to favor and protect as
your children.
Grant that with the help of your love I may despise
all earthly consolation and cling to heavenly
things, until through the Holy Spirit, your faithful Spouse, and through you, His faithful spouse,
Jesus Christ be formed within me for the glory of
the Father. Amen.

*Saint Louis de Montfort (c. 1673–1716)*

Holy Mother Mary swaddles her children in her own virtues
and merits. Their sin is subsumed by grace, their suffering by
joy and glory as Mother Mary tenderly places each of her dear
little children into the depths of divine mercy within the Sacred
Heart of Jesus, a realm of dazzling splendor beyond definition.

### PRAYER TO MARY FOR DIVINE MERCY

Intercede for us, O Mother most pure.
Come to us now in our need.
We are exiles on this earth.
Without end, ever before our eyes,

and even now we perish.
Help us by your prayers, O Merciful Mother.
Be always our advocate lest we are lost
by our own mean spiritedness.
Blessed and most holy one,
plead for us before God
that divine mercy be ours through you.
Amen.

*Maronite Antiochene Rite*

In her diary, Saint Faustina, apostle of the Divine Mercy, gives this prayer to Mary that leads us to the depths of the most merciful Sacred Heart of Jesus.

O Mary, Immaculate Virgin,
pure crystal for my heart,
you are my strength, O sturdy anchor!
You are the weak heart's shield and protection.

O Mary, you are pure, of purity incomparable.
At once both Virgin and Mother,
you are beautiful as the sun, without blemish,
and your soul is beyond all comparison.

Your beauty has delighted the eye of the Thrice-
Holy One.
He descended from heaven, leaving His eternal
throne,
and took Body and Blood of your heart
and for nine months lay hidden in your virgin
womb.

O Mother, Virgin, purest of all lilies,
your heart was Jesus' first tabernacle on earth.
Only because no humility was deeper than yours
were you raised above the choirs of Angels and
above all Saints.

O Mary, my sweet Mother,
I give you my soul, my body, and my poor heart.
Be the guardian of my life,
especially at the hour of death, in the final strife.[13]

*Saint Faustina (c. 1905-1935)*

Saint Ambrose is one of four original Doctors of the Church. Educated in Rome in the fourth century, he was a Bishop and spiritual mentor of Saint Monica. His wisdom and refined intellectual dexterity were influential in the conversion of her illustrious son Augustine, Saint and Doctor of the Church.

## PRAYER FOR MERCIFUL AWARENESS

May the life of Blessed Mary be ever present to
   our awareness.

In her, as in a mirror, the form of virtue and beauty
   of chastity shine forth.

She was virgin, not only in body, but in mind and
   spirit.

She never sullied the pure affection of her heart by
   unworthy feelings.

She was humble of heart.

She was serious in her conversations.

She was prudent in her counsels.

She preferred to pray rather than to speak.

She united in her heart the prayers of the poor

And avoided the uncertainty of worldly riches.

She was ever faithful to her daily duties,

Reserved in her conversations, and always

Accustomed to recognizing God as the Witness of
   her thoughts.

Blessed be the Name of Jesus.

Amen.

*Saint Ambrose, (c. 340-397)*

## PRAYER FOR TRUE WISDOM

O Mary, Mother of God
You were foretold by the Prophets,
Foreshadowed in types and figures
By the Patriarchs,
Described by the Evangelists,
Saluted most graciously by the angels,
Lead us to wisdom of the Presence of God
Now and forever. Amen.

*Saint Sophronius (c. 560-638)*
*Patriarch of Jerusalem*

## PRAYER FOR KNOWLEDGE AND VIRTUE

O Young Mother! O Girl and Mother free!
O bush unburned, burning in Moses' sight!
You came down to us from the Deity,
Through humbleness the Holy Spirit did alight
Upon your heart, whence, through God's might,
You conceived our Father's only Son.
Help me to speak of this with reverence
Holy Lady, your goodness, your magnificence,
Your virtue, and your great humility
Surpass all science and all utterance.

For sometimes, Holy Lady,
Even before people pray to you,
You come to us in your kindness
To bring Light to our prayer,
To be our guide unto your dear Son
Who is so precious to us.

My knowledge is so weak, O blissful Queen,
To speak globally of your mighty worthiness,
That the weight of your virtue is beyond my
        capacity to articulate.
But as a child of twelve months old, or less,
Who labors language to express,
Even so fare I; and therefore, I pray to you,
Guide my words, which I of you shall say.

*Author unknown, (c. 570)*

## PRAYER FOR UNION WITH
## THE SACRAMENT OF LOVE

O Mary, Mother of God
The Divine Sacrament is the most powerful,
And sovereign remedy of all our spiritual miseries.
It is the Source of heavenly comfort to
Alleviate the sorrows of our mortal pilgrimage.

O Mary, Mother of God,
Give to me a deep sense of my spiritual indigence.
Grant, by the power of your motherly intercession
That I may eagerly cry out
"If I but touch the hem of His garment,
I shall be saved!"

Dare I slight the tender invitations of
Our Divine Redeemer?
Dare I disobey His repeated commands,
And disdain His threats?

Show me Holy Mother of God
That I cannot love Jesus
When I do not unite myself with Him
In His Sacrament of Love. Amen.

*Author unknown, (c. 1050)*

### PRAYER TO

### OUR LADY OF WALSINGHAM

O alone of all women, Mother and Virgin,
Mother most happy, Virgin most pure,
we salute thee, we honor thee as how we may
with our humble offerings.
May thy Son grant us that imitating thy most
holy manners,

we also by the grace of the Holy Spirit
may deserve spiritually to conceive Jesus
in our inmost soul,
and once conceived, never to lose Him.
Our Lady of Walsingham, pray for us.
*Desiderius Erasmus Roterodamus (c. 1466-1536)*

## PRAYER FOR HUMILITY

I come to thee, glorious Mother of God, whom
the Church of the Saints call Mother of Humility,
Mother of Mercy. Thou art she, O Mary, who has
never refused the company of anyone; whose
mercy has never failed anyone, or whose clemency
rejected any supplicant. God forbid, mediatrix of
men, and their only hope, after thy Son, that my
sins should be an obstacle to exercising towards me
thy merciful office. Ah, no; assuredly, I hope that
thou wilt deign to obtain for me the grace to expiate
them, to repent of them sincerely. Amen.
*Saint William of Paris (c. 1148–1203)*

Sacred Scripture tells us this is the prayer Mary prayed when the
Word was made flesh and dwelt within her for our salvation.

## MARY'S PRAYER: THE MAGNIFICAT

My soul doth magnify the Lord;

And my spirit hath rejoiced in God my Savior,

Because he hath regarded the humility of his
handmaid;

for behold, from henceforth all generations shall
call me blessed.

Because he that is mighty, hath done great things
to me;

and holy is his name.

And his mercy is from generation unto generation
to them that fear him.

He hath shewed might in his arm:

he hath scattered the proud in the conceit of their
heart.

He hath put down the mighty from their seat,

and hath exalted the humble.

He hath filled the hungry with good things;

and the rich he has sent away empty.

He hath received Israel his servant,

being mindful of his mercy:

as he spoke to our fathers,

to Abraham and to his seed forever.

*Luke 1:46–55*

## CHAPTER 6

# MOTHER OF PERPETUAL HELP

*Prayers and Two Novena for God's Divine Help and Protection*

In A.D. 370, Saint Ephraim of Edessa, Doctor and Father of both the Eastern Orthodox and Roman Catholic Churches, reminded followers of Christ that All-Holy Mary's name is the key to the Gates of Heaven. He prophesied about times when the evil one would deceive the foolish that they are so "blessed" they can enter Heaven without the key.

Christ alone brings beauty and fulfillment to the deepest longings of every human heart. No one knows this better than His Mother Mary. Christ through Mary is not about bypassing God or offending the Lord Jesus. Rather, Mother Mary's intercessory prayer is perfectly pleasing to God and allows our needs and desires to be presented by our Heavenly Mother in the most favorable light.

No creature can get to God, manipulate God, or force God. God alone is Perfection. God needs nothing. Every prayer of ours draws a measure of God's perfection upon us.

Mysteriously, God longs for our response to His unfathomable, unquenchable love for us. That is the impenetrable mystery of Mother Mary's role in the Incarnation of the Second Person of the Most Holy Trinity.[1] It is God, in His divine mercy, who reaches out and grasps His human creature.[2] He did that by means of the Virgin Mary whose faith-filled obedience to God's Plan gave us Jesus Christ who is Divine Mercy Incarnate.[3]

Mother Mary is fully human: she knows all the joys and sorrows we carry. When Mother Mary consented to Christmas Day, she also consented to Good Friday and the Resurrection on Easter Sunday. Our Heavenly Mother Mary's heart is so filled with tender compassion and unconditional love for us that she freely takes much of our cup of adversity that life brings and drinks it herself, saving for us only the sweeter portion. It is God's great love for us, and Mother Mary's great love for God that draw Christ's Mother into the most difficult moments of our life. God allows Himself to be touched by His own Mother's tears on our behalf. Although Mother Mary's children too must suffer, their suffering is different. Faithful children of Christ's Mother persevere hidden and safe within the sanctified folds of the mantle of the Queen Mother of Heaven.

Most of us are aware of our lack of perfection. Our Christian ancestors taught us to turn to God's human Mother Mary who was supernaturally assumed into heaven for help in knowing, loving and serving God as He requires. It is natural for faithful followers of Christ to approach His Heavenly Mother for protection and guidance. When we remember to do so, All-Holy Mary gently helps us love and trust her Son Jesus more, understand His ways in our present circumstances, and find the joy of God's Plan for our unique life. Even in the most adverse circumstances, we are always blessed in God's perfect Plan He ordained for us from all eternity. There is no other safety. There is no other blessing.

In this chapter are two famous and powerful novenas enlisting Mother Mary's protection. Novenas, which are prayed for many reasons, date back to the foundation of the Church as a popular practice developed to honor the nine months that Jesus Christ spent in the womb of His Blessed Mother. Some cultures also pray special novenas to honor the nine days that the apostles, disciples and Mother Mary prayed in the Upper Room between the Ascension of Jesus Christ and the Coming of the Holy Spirit at Pentecost.

A novena is a prayer or series of prayers that is said on nine consecutive occasions. Often people pray novenas daily or once a week or once a month for nine days or weeks or months and sometimes on a designated day or date. Some pray a novena once an hour.

Novenas are quite efficacious, especially when they are said in groups, whether in church or a prayer group or among family or friends. In addition to praying the novena, the faithful are encouraged to attend daily Mass and receive the Holy Eucharist, or to otherwise participate in whatever worship service is appropriate and available. A powerful accompaniment to any novena is some kind of hidden penance, fasting and almsgiving added to the daily routine solely for the love of God. The effects of such prayer commitment, strengthened by penance, fasting and almsgiving are oftentimes extraordinary. Consequently, novenas are popular all over the world.

Mary is always our "Mother Most Faithful". She humbly but surely guides us to fully accept Jesus Christ's scriptural path to God. Our Heavenly Mother helps us to find peace and fulfillment in what some consider littleness and simplicity. The irony is that faithful participants in God's infinite Plan are infinitely blessed. Our Heavenly Mother shows us how to willingly cooperate with God's unique Plan for our life and allow the Most Holy Trinity to dwell in us in fullness. Mother Mary helps us create a tiny chapel within our hearts for the Lord. Our love for Him is our votive lamp.

God's ways are not always our ways, but they are the best ways. When we desire special help and protection, all we need to do is sincerely ask our Heavenly Mother Most Faithful to guide us into the Sacred Heart of her Son hidden within the interior kingdom of our souls.

### PRAYER TO MARY FOR PEACE, SECURITY, AND MATERIAL NEEDS

Hail, Lady of the world, and Heaven's bright Queen
Virgin of Virgins hail,

You are serene in God.
You shine over the earth in the early morning Light
Filled with celestial grace, and Light divine.
O Lady of God
Hasten and extend over us your loving arms.
May your celestial grace guard us from evil.
May your Light divine defend us from all our enemies.
Amen.

*Adapted from the Office of the Blessed Virgin Mary*

### PRAYER OF A PARENT FOR A CHILD

Ave Maria! maiden mild,
Listen to a maiden's prayer.
Thou canst hear, though from the wild.
Thou canst save amidst despair.
Safe may we sleep beneath thy care,
Though banished, outcast, and reviled—
Maiden! hear a maiden's prayer,
Mother! hear a suppliant child! Ave Maria!

Ave Maria! undefiled!
The flinty couch we now must share,
Shall seem with down of eider piled,
If thy protection hover there.
The murky cavern's heavy air

Shall breathe of balm if thou hast smiled,
Then Maiden! hear a maiden's prayer.
Mother! listen to a suppliant child! Ave Maria!

Ave Maria! stainless styled,
Foul demons of the earth and air,
From this their wonted haunt exiled
Shall flee before thy presence fair.
We bow us to our lot of care
Beneath thy guidance reconciled.
Hear for a maid a maiden's prayer,
And for a father hear a child. Ave Maria!

*Sir Walter Scott (c. 1771–1832)*

## PRAYER FOR ANGELIC PROTECTION

August Queen of Heaven, sovereign Mistress of the
  Angels,
who did receive from the beginning the mission
  and power to crush the serpent's head,
we beseech thee to send thy holy angels, that
  under thy command,
and by thy power they may pursue the evil spirits,
encounter them on every side, resist their bold
  attacks, and drive them hence into the abyss
  of woe.

Most Holy Mother send thy angels to defend us
   and drive the cruel enemy from us.
All ye holy angels and archangels, help
   and defend us.
O good and tender Mother! Thou shalt ever be
   our love and hope.
Holy Angels and Archangels, keep and defend us.
Amen.[4]

## PRAYER FOR PROTECTION
## AGAINST DEMONS

O Mary, powerful Virgin,

You are the mighty and glorious Protector of the
   Church.

You are the Marvelous Help of Christians.

You are Terrible as an Army set in Battle Array.

You alone have destroyed every heresy in the entire
   Church.

In the midst of my anguish, my struggles and my
   distress,

Defend me from the power of the enemy,

And at the hour of my death,

Receive my soul into Paradise.

*Saint John Bosco, (c. 1880)*

## MOTHER OF PERPETUAL HELP PRAYER

Mother dearest, mother fairest
Help of all who call on thee,
Virgin purest, brightest, rarest,
Help us, help, we cry to thee.
Free us from all sin and sadness,
Fill our hearts with peace, with gladness.
Mary, Mother, help away!
Mary, Virgin, help us aye!

Lady, help in pain and sorrow
Soothe those racked on bed of pain,
May the golden light of morrow
Bring them health and joy again,
Bring them health and joy again.

Help the poor, the sad, the weary,
Comfort those whose homes are dreary.
Mary, Mother, help away!
Mary, Virgin, help us aye!

Mother! Help the absent loved ones,
Ah! We miss their presence here!
Help them, guard them far and near.
Save them from all sin and danger,

Lead safe home the weary stranger,
Mary, Mother, help away!
Mary, Virgin, help us aye!

Mother, help the wounded soldier,
Set the pining captive free,
Help the sailor on mid-ocean,
Help those in their agony,
From the demon's malice, guard them,
In their death-pangs, watch and ward them.
Mary, Mother, help away!
Mary, Virgin, pray! Oh pray!

Help our priests, our virgins holy,
Help our Pope—Long may he reign!
Pray that we who sing thy praises,
May in heaven all meet again.
Help us when our life grows dreary,
Thy heart too was sad and weary,
Mary, Mother, help away!
Mary, Virgin, pray! Oh pray!

*Author unknown, (c. 1890)*

## PRAYER FOR
## GOD'S DIVINE PROTECTION

O Mother All Merciful, thou hast come to us with
outstretched hands, overflowing with graces, in order
to attract us to thyself, and to load us with favors.
We hasten, therefore, to follow the odor of thy
perfumes, sweeter far than that of roses. Gird us
with the cord of purity and penance, cover us with
the veil of modesty, bind us to thy service with the
links of a faithful love, and lay upon our breasts the
blessed Scapular of the Heart of thy Divine Son.
May it be for us henceforth the pledge of thy most
powerful protection until the day when we shall rest
at last in the bosom of God for all eternity. Amen.

*With the approbation of*
*the Archbishop of Bourges*

The following novena is extremely effective and has been prayed
by many generations of families. One should be quite certain
to truly desire that for which this novena is prayed each day for
thirty days. If at the end of thirty days you have not received what
you are praying for, continue to say the novena. It has never been
known to fail. A remarkable side effect of this noble novena is
personal growth in holiness.

## THIRTY DAYS' NOVENA PRAYER TO THE BLESSED VIRGIN MARY

*Commemorative of the Passion of Our Lord Jesus Christ.*

Ever glorious and blessed Mary, Queen of Virgins, Mother of Mercy, hope and comfort of dejected and desolate souls,

through the sword of sorrow which pierced thy tender heart, whilst thine only Son, our Lord Jesus Christ suffered ignominy and death upon the cross;

through that filial tenderness and pure love He had for thee, grieving in thy grief, whilst from His cross He recommended thee to the care and protection of His beloved disciple, St. John,

have pity upon us, we beseech thee, on our poverty and necessities; have compassion on our anxieties.

Assist and comfort us in all our infirmities and miseries.

Thou art the Mother of Mercy, the sweet consolatrix and refuge of the desolate and afflicted:

look therefore with pity on us, miserable children of Eve, and hear our prayer: for since, in just punishment for our sins, we are encompassed by evils, whither can we fly for more secure shelter than to thy maternal protection?

Attend, therefore, with an ear of pity, we beseech thee, to our humble and earnest request.

We ask it through the mercy of Jesus Christ, thy Son, the Redeemer of the world.

We ask it through the anguish of mind wherewith thy beloved Son, our dear Savior, was overwhelmed on Mount Olivet, when He besought His Eternal Father to remove from Him, if possible, the bitter chalice of His future Passion.

We ask it through the threefold repetition of His prayer in the garden, from whence afterwards, with mournful tears, thou didst accompany Him along the doleful Stations of His sufferings and death.

We ask it through the welts and sores of His virginal flesh, occasioned by the cords and whips wherewith He was bound and scourged when stripped of His seamless garment, for which His executioners afterwards cast lots.

We ask it through the scoffs and ignominies by which He was insulted, the false accusations, and unjust sentence by which He was condemned to death, and which He bore with heavenly patience.

We ask it through His bitter tears and sweat of blood, His silence and resignation, His sadness and grief of heart.

We ask it through the blood which trickled from His royal and sacred head, when struck with the scepter of a reed and pierced with His crown of thorns.

We ask it through the torments He endured, when His hands and feet were cruelly fastened to the tree of the cross.

We ask it through His vehement thirst and bitter potion of vinegar and gall.

We ask it through His dereliction on the cross, when He exclaimed: "My God, My God, why hast Thou forsaken Me?"

We ask it through His mercy extended to the good thief, and through His recommending His precious soul into the hands of His Eternal Father before He expired, saying: "All is consummated."

We ask it through the blood mixed with water which issued from His sacred side when pierced with a lance, and whence a flood of grace and mercy hath flowed upon us.

We ask it through His immaculate life, bitter Passion, and ignominious death upon the cross, at which nature itself was thrown into convulsions, by the bursting of rocks, rending of the veil of the Temple, the earthquake, and darkness of the sun and moon.

We ask it through His descent to the dead where He comforted the saints of the Old Law and led captivity captive.

We ask it through His glorious victory over death, His triumphant ascension into Heaven, and through the grace of the Holy Spirit, infused into the hearts of the disciples when He descended upon them in the form of fiery tongues.

We ask it through His awful appearance on the Last Day, when He shall come to judge the living and the dead.

We ask it through the compassion He bore thee, and the ineffable joy thou didst feel at thine assumption into heaven, where thou art eternally absorbed in the sweet contemplation of His Divine Perfections.

O glorious and ever blessed Virgin, comfort the hearts of thy supplicants, by obtaining for us . . . (*Here mention your request.*)

And as we are persuaded that our Divine Savior honors thee as His beloved Mother, to whom He can refuse nothing because thou asketh nothing contrary to His Divine Will, so let us speedily experience the efficacy of thy powerful intercession, according to the tenderness of thy maternal affection, and the charity of His amiable Heart, which mercifully granteth the requests, and complieth with the desires of those who love and fear Him.

O most Blessed Virgin, besides the object of our present petition, and whatever else we may stand in need of, obtain for us of thy dear Son, our Lord and our God, lively faith, firm hope, perfect charity, true contrition, a horror of sin, love of God and our neighbor, contempt of the world, and patience and resignation under the trials and difficulties of this life.

Obtain for us, O sacred Mother of God, the gift of final perseverance, and the grace to receive the last sacraments worthily at the hour of death.

Lastly obtain, we beseech thee, for our parents, siblings, spouse, children, grandchildren, great grandchildren, godchildren, relatives, friends, forbears, progeny, our benefactors, and all those we influence remotely or proximately, whether living, dead or yet to be born, life everlasting. Amen.[5]

The world-renowned Miraculous Medal Novena, like its counterpart the Miraculous Medal have sustained generations of Mary's children of all nations and stations in life.

### NOVENA PRAYER TO OUR LADY OF THE MIRACULOUS MEDAL

O Immaculate Virgin Mary, Mother of Our Lord Jesus and our Mother, penetrated with the liveliest confidence in your all-powerful and never-failing intercession, manifested so often through the Miraculous Medal, we, your loving and trusting children implore you to obtain for us the graces and favors we ask during this Novena, if they be beneficial to our immortal souls, and the souls for whom we pray. (*Here privately form your petitions.*) You know, O Mary, how often our souls have been the sanctuaries of your Son who hates iniquity. Obtain for us then a deep hatred of sin and that purity of heart which will attach us to God alone so that our every thought, word and deed may tend to His greater glory. Obtain for us also a spirit of prayer and self-denial that we may recover by penance what we have lost by sin and at length attain to that blessed abode where you are Queen of Angels and of Saints. Amen.

### CONSECRATION PRAYER TO OUR LADY OF THE MIRACULOUS MEDAL

O Virgin Mother of God, Mary Immaculate, we dedicate and consecrate ourselves to you under the title of Our Lady of the Miraculous Medal. May this medal be for each one of us a sure sign of your affection for us and a constant reminder of our duties toward you. Ever while wearing it, may we be blessed by your loving protection and preserved in the grace of your Son. O most powerful Virgin, Mother of our Savior, keep us close to you every moment of our lives. Obtain for us, your children, the grace of a happy death; so that in union with you, we may enjoy the bliss of Heaven forever. Amen.

O Mary, conceived without sin, pray for us who have recourse to you. Amen.

## CHAPTER 7

# MOTHER OF GOOD COUNCIL

*Prayers in Times of Stress, Sorrow, Illness, Difficulties, and Abandonment*

As each new season brings celebrations that honor the victories of Mary's Son, Jesus the Christ, over the evils of the world, each season also brings disappointments and difficulties. Who knows better how to comfort us during difficult times than Holy Mother Mary who dwelt near her dying Son, our Redeemer? Whose heart is more overflowing with unconditional love for God's children?

If we ask our Blessed Mother to help us in our times of trouble, our Heavenly Mother takes our cup of sorrow and drinks deeply from it, spoon-feeding us only a small amount. Blessed Mother Mary always brings her Son Jesus the Christ to help us; He is the Redeemer who heals all the evils in the world.[1]

Illness, sorrow, abandonment and stress of all kinds bring not only grief but the opportunity to pray. Our prayers at such times need not be complex. A prayer can be a simple outpouring from our heart toward the person, situation, or event for whom or which a divine remedy is desired. Consider the following handed-down history of the power of one simple prayer to our Heavenly Mother Mary that rescued an entire city.

It is said that during the reign of Doctor of the Church Pope Saint Gregory the Great (c. 590–604), human hearts had grown hard and cynical. A devastating plague broke out in Rome. Vast numbers of people succumbed to the ravages of the highly contagious epidemic, suffered horribly and died violently. The stench of death was everywhere. Medical science had no remedy for the plague.

The Pope, walking barefoot on a chilly Easter morning, turned in prayer to All-Holy Mary as Mother of God and Queen of Heaven and Earth. In a public act of faith and defiant of the plague that was wiping out the population of Rome, Pope Saint Gregory carried a sacred icon, reputedly painted by Saint Luke, in solemn procession from the Church of Saint Mary Major to Saint Peter's Basilica.

Family stories survive even to these times that those who witnessed the solemn procession heard angelic choirs chanting the glorious Resurrection Hymn that acknowledges and praises God's gifts to All- Holy Mary for all of us. People stooped with sorrow and pain were suddenly filled with joy at the sound of angels on high. They joined their voices with the angels to pray this prayer.

### PRAYER IN TIME OF DISASTER
### QUEEN OF HEAVEN
### (*REGINA COELI*)

O Queen of Heaven, rejoice, Alleluia,
For He Whom you were privileged to bear,
    Alleluia,
Has risen, as He said, Alleluia.
Pray for us to God, Alleluia. Rejoice and be glad,
O Virgin Mary,
Alleluia.

For the Lord has risen indeed,
Alleluia.

Let us pray.
O God, Who gave joy to the world
Through the resurrection of Your Son,
Our Lord Jesus Christ;
Grant, we beseech You
That through His Mother, the Virgin Mary,
We may obtain the joys of everlasting life.
Through the same Christ our Lord.
Amen.
May the Divine Assistance remain always with us.
Amen.[2]

The crowds grew as sounds of the angelic hosts on high filled the area with the music of Heaven. The sick and dying were brought to the site.

Suddenly, a huge warrior angel brandishing an avenging sword over the population was visible in the sky. People fell to their knees in shock, fright, and deadly fear. Slowly the crowds joined their voices with the Pontiff praying the *Queen of Heaven Prayer* over and over again with contagious devotion.

As he knelt before the sacred icon, Pope Saint Gregory was demonstrating to the crowds that a person worships God by laying down his or her agenda at every moment in favor of God's agenda. Truth is that our human agenda is limitation at work, but God's agenda is divinity at work. The avenging angel's fierce sword reminded everyone of God's sacred truth written upon each human heart. Humankind enjoys divine protection by cooperation with God's loving Plan. There is no other protection.

As people prayed the *Queen of Heaven Prayer*, they numinously perceived the way Jesus Christ, through His All-Holy Mother Mary, obeyed our Heavenly Father's Plan for the salvation of His prodigal children. This encounter with sacred truth contained divine light to recognize that our Heavenly Father created and prepared Mary to be the immaculate mother of His only begotten Son Jesus the Christ for the redemption of all humanity. It is said everyone saw the Angel of Chastisement replace his sword of vengeance in his scabbard as people consented to imbibe this sacred truth. The sick got well. There were no further reported cases of plague.

That generation and those after them would never forget the Angel of Chastisement for they had seen him with their own eyes or heard eyewitness accounts. People spoke of God's Plan for humanity with renewed reverence and taught their children to obey God's Commandments. They remembered and respected the blessings they carried through their baptism and sacramental life. Thereafter, All-Holy Mary, most faithful of all God's creatures, was highly honored in music, art, theater, architecture, and literature. Humanity was gradually learning that to praise Mother Mary is to praise God's immutable Plan to redeem the human race; to honor her is to imitate her virtues. The *Queen of Heaven Prayer* of praise continues to be prayed by the faithful, and most especially in times of great need or celebration.

A chapel dedicated to Saint Michael the Archangel, who is known as the Guardian Angel of Mary, was built at the site where Pope Saint Gregory the Great led the population of Rome in public recitation of the *Queen of Heaven Prayer*. The ancient figure of God's Angel of Chastisement, carved in white marble, stands, even now, in the proximity of Saint Mary Major Church in Rome.

The following sacred anthem of the Blessed Virgin Mary comes to us from the early days of the Church. It has a glorious history and brings wonderful blessings and unexpected miracles, especially in times of sorrow, illness, betrayal, and abandonment.

## PRAYER IN TIMES OF SORROW, ILLNESS, ABANDONMENT
### (*ALMA REDEMPTORIS*)

Mother of Christ, hear your people's cry,
Star of the deep and portal of the sky.
Mother of the One Who made you
from nothing
In our strivings we struggle and call to you
for aid.
O by that joy which Gabriel the Archangel
brought to you
Pure Virgin, first and last
Look on our misery. Amen.

*Herman the Cripple (c. 1013-1054)*
*Translation: Rev. Edward Caswall 1849*

The following prayer, though of ancient origin, has a remarkable history of heavenly aid in times of distress, betrayal, failure, and bitterness. It is said that the joy this prayer evokes in heaven spills over the earth bringing unexpected abundance.

## PRAYER IN DISTRESS, PAIN, BETRAYAL, FAILURE, BITTERNESS
### (*AVE REGINA COELORUM*)

Hail Queen of Heaven enthroned!
Hail Queen of all the angels!
Root of Jesse! Gate of Morning,
From whom the world's True Light
Was born:
Glorious Virgin, joy to you,
You are beautiful beyond compare!
Fairest of all God's creation
Speak on our behalf a loving prayer.
Grant that we may praise you
O Blessed Virgin,
Give us strength against our enemies.

Let us pray.
O Most Merciful God,
Grant us help in our weaknesses,
That as we celebrate the memory of the
    All-Holy Mother of God,
So, by the help of her intercession
May we rise again from the pain of our mistakes
Through the same Christ Our Lord. Amen.[3]

A prayer to Mary by Doctor of the Church, Saint Theresa of Lisieux, is filled with wisdom for all times.

### THE LITTLE FLOWER'S
### PRAYER TO MARY

Virgin full of grace,
I know that at Nazareth you lived modestly, with-
out requesting anything more.
Neither ecstasies, nor miracles, nor other
    extraordinary deeds enhanced your life
O Queen of the Elect.
The number of the lowly, "little ones," is very
great on earth.
They can raise their eyes to you without any fear.
You are the incomparable Mother
who walks with them along the common way
to guide them to heaven.

Beloved Mother,
in this harsh exile,
I want to live always with you
and follow you every day.
I am enraptured by the contemplation of you
and I discover the depths of the love of your
Heart.

All my fears vanish under your Motherly gaze,
which teaches me to weep and rejoice![4]
*Saint Theresa of the Child Jesus (c. 1874-1879)*

The beautiful *Litany of Loreto* honors Mary, the Mother of God under many sacred titles. Throughout the centuries it has been prayed as a type of stepping-stone in the journey to union with God. Some choose a special title from this Litany for meditation each day. Others appropriate a special title as a guide for their lives, or for a project, military campaign, building, event, work of art or music, or as patroness of a city, state, or nation.

Each stanza, fervently prayed, deepens human humility and plants seeds of wisdom that, properly nourished, grow into a well-lit ramp to the Gate of Heaven. Although this Litany is often prayed in churches as a dialogue between congregation and priest, or other prayer leader, it is quite effective when prayed alone.

Lord, *have mercy on us.*
*Lord, have mercy on us.*
Christ have mercy on us.
*Christ have mercy on us.*
Lord, have mercy on us.
*Lord, have mercy on us.*
Christ *hear us.*
*Christ graciously hear us.*

God the Father of heaven *have mercy on us.*
God the Son, Redeemer of the world, *have mercy
   on us.*
God the Holy Spirit *have mercy on us.*
Holy Trinity, one God, *have mercy on us.*

Mary, *pray for us.*
Holy Mother of God *pray for us.*
Mother of Christ *pray for us.*
Mother of Divine Grace, *pray for us.*
Mother of the Church pray *for us.*
Mother Most Pure, *pray for us.*
Mother Most Chaste, *pray for us.*
Mother Inviolate, *pray for us.*
Mother Undefiled, *pray for us.*
Mother Most Lovable, *pray for us.*
Mother Most Admirable, *pray for us.*
Mother of Good Counsel *pray for us.*
Mother of Our Creator *pray for us.*
Mother of Our Savior pray *for us.*

Virgin Most Prudent, *pray for us.*
Virgin Most Venerable, *pray for us.*
Virgin Most Renowned, *pray for us.*
Virgin Most Powerful, *pray for us.*
Virgin Most Merciful, *pray for us.*
Virgin Most Faithful, *pray for us.*

Mirror of Justice *pray for us.*
Seat of Wisdom *pray for us.*
Cause of Our Joy, *pray for us.*
Spiritual Vessel *pray for us.*
Vessel of Honor *pray for us.*
Singular Vessel of Devotion *pray for us.*
Mystical Rose, *pray for us.*
Tower of David, *pray for us.*
Tower of Ivory *pray for us.*
House of Gold *pray for us.*
Ark of the Covenant *pray for us.*
Gate of Heaven *pray for us.*
Morning Star *pray for us.*
Health of the Sick, *pray for us.*
Refuge of Sinners *pray for us.*
Comfort of the Afflicted, *pray for us.*
Help of God's People, *pray for us.*

Queen of Patriarchs *pray for us.*
Queen of Angels *pray for us.*
Queen of Prophets *pray for us.*
Queen of Apostles *pray for us.*
Queen of Martyrs *pray for us.*
Queen of Confessors *pray for us.*
Queen of Virgins *pray for us.*
Queen of All Saints *pray for us.*
Queen Conceived Without Original Sin, *pray
    for us.*

Queen Assumed into Heaven *pray for us.*
Queen of the Most Holy Rosary *pray for us.*
Queen of Peace *pray for us.*

Lamb of God, You take away the sins of the world,
    *spare us O Lord.*
Lamb of God, You take away the sins of the world,
    *graciously hear us, O Lord.*
Lamb of God, You take away the sins of the world,
    *have mercy on us.*
Pray for us, O Holy Mother of God,
That we may be made worthy of the promises of
    Christ.

Let us pray.

Lord God, give to Your people the joy of
continual health in mind, body, and spirit. With the
prayers of the Blessed Virgin Mary to help us,
guide us through the sorrows of this life to eternal
happiness now and in the life to come. Grant this
through our Lord, Jesus Christ, Your Son, Who lives
and reigns with You and the Holy Spirit, one God, for
ever and ever. Amen.

## SODALITY PRAYER IN TIMES OF DARKNESS

Mother dear, O pray for me,
whilst far from heaven and thee
I wander in a fragile bark
O'er life's tempestuous sea.
O Virgin Mother, from thy throne
so bright in bliss above,
Protect thy child and cheer my path
With thy sweet smile of love.

Mother dear, remember me,
and never cease thy care,
Till in heaven eternally
Thy love and bliss I share.

Mother dear, O pray for me,
Should pleasure's siren lay
E'er tempt thy child to wander far
from virtue's path away.
When thorns beset life's devious way,
And darkling waters flow,
Then, Mary, aid thy needy child,
Thyself a mother show.

*Sodality Manual*

## PRAYER TO ELIMINATE FEAR

O Mother of God, if I place my confidence in you,
I shall be saved.
If I am under your protection,
I have nothing to fear,
for the fact of being your child is the possession of a
  certainty of salvation,
which God grants only to those He intends to save.

*Saint John Damascene, (c. 749)*

## PRAYER IN BETRAYAL

Virgin, gentlest of all God's creatures,
show me how you acted toward the many
    ungrateful people
whom Jesus taught and for whom He worked
    great miracles.
Thus, I shall learn how to endure the faults of
    my neighbor.
How often you witnessed the ingratitude and
    betrayal Jesus received in turn for the good
    He did!
Yet your thoughts and feelings toward His
    enemies were,
like His, only thoughts and feelings of peace.
You detested sin, but you loved the sinner.

It was only the offense against God that moved
    you deeply;
you let no complaint against these foolish ones
    pass your lips, and you even took up their
    cause with Jesus.
You acted toward them as you now act, after so
    many years, toward me.
I am the most faithless and ungrateful of your
    servants,
yet you treat me with kindness and win ever new
    favors from God for me.
Mother of the God of peace, win for me the grace
    never again to distress anyone with unkind
    words.
Your very name and image cause me to think
    mild thoughts.
Obtain for me the virtue of gentleness and the
    spirit of peace,
so that I may merit the glorious title of "child of
    God."[5]

*Alexander De Rouville, S.J., (c.1768)*

### PRAYER IN TIME OF TRIAL

All-holy Lady,
do not abandon me to the power of human beings.

Hear the plea of your servant
for I am oppressed by anguish
and find it difficult to resist the pressures of evil.
I have no defense
and I do not know where to flee.
I am assailed on all sides
and I find no consolation except in you.
Queen of the world,
hope and protection of the faithful,
do not despise my petition
but grant me what I need.

*Byzantine Liturgy*

## PRAYER FOR MERCY, PITY, AND KINDNESS

O Virgin Mother, daughter of your Son,
humble and exalted beyond every creature,
and established term of God's eternal Plan,

you are the one who ennobled human nature
to such an extent that its Divine Maker
did not disdain to become its workmanship. . .

O Lady, you are so great and powerful
that those who seek grace without recourse to you
are expecting wishes to fly without wings.

Your loving kindness not only comes to the aid
of those who ask for it but very often spontaneously
precedes the request for it.

In you is mercy, in you is pity,
in you is magnificence, in you is found
everything that is good in God's creation.

*Dante,* Paradiso, *canto XXXIII (c. 1265-1321)*

## PRAYER IN STRESS AND SORROW

Kneeling at thy feet, O gracious Queen of Heaven,
we offer thee our deepest reverence. Thou art the
daughter of the Eternal Father, the mother of the
Divine Word, and the spouse of the Holy Spirit. Full
of grace, of virtue, and of heavenly gifts, thou art
the chaste temple of God's mercies. Thy loving heart
is filled with charity, sweetness and tender compassion for poor sinners, and we call thee Mother of
Holy Pity. With the utmost trust I come to thee in
my sorrow and distress. Give me confidence in thy
love, and grant me what I ask— if it be God's will,
and for the welfare of my soul. Cast thine eyes of
pity upon me and upon all with whom I am in any
way connected. Shield me from the attacks of the
world, the flesh and the devil. Remember, O fondest

of mothers, that I am thy child, purchased with the precious blood of thy Divine Son. Pray without ceasing that the adorable Trinity may give me the grace ever to triumph over the devil, the world, and my passions. I ask this, O most pure Virgin, through the infinite bounty of the Most Holy God, through the merits of thy Divine Son, by the care with which thou didst nourish Him, by the devotion with which thou didst serve Him, by the love with which thou didst cherish Him, by thy tears and anguish in the days of thy pilgrimage. Obtain that the whole world may be made one people and one church, which shall give thanks, praise and glory to the Most Holy Trinity, and to thee who art its mediator.

May the power of the Father, the wisdom of the Son and the virtue of the Holy Spirit grant us this blessing. Amen.

*Pope Pius IX, c. 1860*

## PRAYER TO OUR LADY OF LOURDES FOR HEALING

O ever Immaculate Virgin, Mother of Mercy,
Health of the Sick, Refuge of Sinners, Comfort of
the Afflicted,
You know my wants, my troubles, my sufferings.

Deign to cast upon me a look of mercy.
By appearing in the Grotto of Lourdes,
You were pleased to make it a privileged sanctuary
Where you dispense your favors.
Already many sufferers have obtained the cure
of their infirmities both spiritual and corporal.
I come, therefore, with unbounded confidence to
    implore
Your maternal intercession.
Obtain, O loving Mother,
the granting of my request . . .
I will endeavor to imitate your virtues
That I may one day share your glories
and bless you in eternity. Amen.[6]

### PRAYER TO ALLEVIATE SUFFERING

O Blessed Virgin Mary, who can worthily speak
    words of praise and thanksgiving to you, for
    the wondrous assent of your will that rescued a
    fallen world?

What songs of praise can our weak human nature
    recite in your honor, since it is by your inter-
    vention alone that it has found the way to
    restoration?

Accept kindly, the poor thanks as we offer to you

now, though insignificant in value to the gift
you have given us.

Dear Mother, receive the commitments we make,
obtain by your prayers the remedies for all our
mistakes.

Carry our prayers within the sanctuary of your
heavenly life with God and bring forth to us
the gift of our reconciliation.

Take our offering, grant us our requests, obtain
pardon for what we fear, for you are the sole
hope of sinners.

Mary, our Mother, help the miserable, strengthen
the fainthearted, comfort the sorrowful, pray
for your people, intercede for the clergy, for all
men, women and children consecrated to God.

Be ever near us and assist us when we pray.

Bring to us always loving answers to our prayers.

Make it your continual commitment to pray for the
people of God, you, who are blessed by God,
who merited to bear the Redeemer of the world

Who lives and reigns, world without end.

Amen.

*Saint Augustine (c. 354–430)*[7]

Few have reached the pinnacles of celestial knowledge that
Carmelite Doctor of the Church Saint Theresa of Avila bequeaths

to humankind. Her prayer that follows is a resource that belongs
to people of all faiths and nations

### PRAYER FOR PERSONAL PEACE

Let nothing disturb you. Let nothing frighten you. All
things are passing. God only is changeless. Patience
gains all things. Whoever has God wants for nothing.
God alone suffices.

*Saint Theresa of Avila (c. 1515-1582)*[8]

The prayer below comforted Pope Leo XIII in his old age when
sorrow and pain surrounded him.

### PRAYER IN SORROW
### AND PAIN OF OLD AGE

As a little child,
I loved you like a Mother.
Now that I am old,
my love for you has grown.

Receive me in heaven
as one of the blessed,

and I will proclaim
that I have obtained
such a great prize
through your patronage.

*Pope Leo XIII (c. 1810–1903)*

## PRAYER FOR THE DYING

O Mary, pierced with sorrow, remember, reach and save
the soul that goes tomorrow before the God that gave
it life. As each was born of woman, from each in utter
need, true friend and brave, blessed lady, Madonna,
intercede. Amen.

*Rudyard Kipling (1865–1936)*

## SAINT THOMAS MORE'S PRAYER
## TO MARY AT DEATH

When evening shades are falling
O'er Ocean's sunnt sleep,
To pilgrim hearts recalling
Their home beyond the deep;
When rest o'er all descending,
The shores with gladness smile,
And lutes their echoes blending,

Are heard from aisle to aisle,
Then, Mary, Star of the Sea,
We pray, we pray to thee.

The noonday tempest over,
Now Ocean toils no more,
And wings of halcyons hover
Where all was strife before.
Oh, thus may life, in closing
Its short tempestuous day,
Beneath Heaven's smile reposing,
Shine all its storms away:
Thus, Mary, Star of the Sea,
We pray, we pray, to thee.

On Helle's sea, the light grew dim,
As the last sounds of that sweet hymn
Floated along its azure tide—
Floated in light as if the lay
Had mixed with sunset's fading ray—
And light and song together died.

*Saint Thomas More (c. 1478–1535)*

## CHAPTER 8

# MOTHER
# MOST LOVABLE

*Prayers for Daily Inspiration*

Certain realities never change. Faith is a highly blessed gift flowing to us from God's infinite love. If we don't appreciate the gift of faith and integrate it more and more into our everyday lives, we fritter it away. God has created us to prayerfully exercise our faith at all times. The prayers to Mary in this chapter help strengthen our faith. Those who enter the Sacred Heart of Jesus Christ through His Mother Mary have access to divine chambers reserved for intimate family members.

An American pilgrim visiting Bethlehem was enjoying all the wares on display in shops along the way to the site of the shrine where the Christ Child was born. Suddenly, the distracted pilgrim noticed Saint Joseph at the top of the small hill overlooking Shepherd's Field. Totally forgetting the shops, the amazed pilgrim scurried up the hill to the entrance of the nativity shrine. The sunlight was blinding. In that cloud of awareness, the pilgrim realized no one ever draws near the Most Holy Mother of God without permission of her Most Sacred Son and His protective, putative father, Saint Joseph. The pilgrim immediately prayed for the Lord's permission to enter the cave shrine. The sunlight became more intense. The pilgrim (who knew little of Saint Joseph) was led to ask Mother Mary's chaste spouse, mysteriously present in the blinding light, for his permission to draw near his wife and her sacred son. The pilgrim bent low to pass through the small opening into the cave that houses the Nativity Shrine. Divine Truth was present there.

During the height of the global Covid-19 pandemic, Pope Francis consecrated the year beginning December 8, 2020 to December 8, 2021 to Saint Joseph who is Patron of the Universal Church. God appointed Saint Joseph personal guardian of the sacred humanity of His only-begotten Son Jesus and His immaculate mother Mary.[1]

Saint Joseph played a highly significant role in the great work of our salvation. Consequently, he is included in the merciful counsels of the Incarnate Wisdom, Jesus the Christ.[2] Imagine the discussions that took place around the kitchen table of the Holy Family in Egypt and Nazareth.

When faith is weak or possibly nonexistent, prayers of inspiration in this chapter present a special opportunity. A mental exercise which uses a technique called interior intellectual imaging sometimes attracts the gift of faith, strengthens it, or restores it. Those who respond to grace by practicing this prayer exercise do best if they sincerely open their hearts to belief in reality beyond the five senses.

Select any prayer or prayers in this chapter that interest you or use any other prayer in the book. Find a quiet place where you will not be disturbed. Picture in your mind the joy of knowing All-Holy Mother Mary who not only loves you unconditionally, just as you are, but also appreciates you and praises God for every fiber of your being. Perhaps in your mind's eye you observe an icon, or other image of Mary holding her Divine Infant Jesus. Visualize yourself as a tiny child along with the Redeemer Christ Child in the arms of Mary, your Heavenly Mother. Perceive that you have a heavenly guardian in Saint Joseph who protects you as part of the Holy Family of the Most Holy Trinity. Focus on the image in your imagination as you say these words: "God, I believe. Please help my unbelief."

Hold on to your interior, intellectual experience of belonging to your unconditionally loving Heavenly Mother Mary and her beloved spouse Saint Joseph. Allow yourself to feel comfortable that you are totally known and unconditionally loved not only by God, who created and redeemed you, but also by Christ's Mother Mary and His putative father Joseph. Choose to believe Mother

Mary, Baby Jesus and Saint Joseph most certainly love you just as you are, watch over you constantly, protect you and pray for you always. Accept the fact that you are indeed a little brother or sister of the only-begotten Son of God. Try to be grateful that your big brother Jesus the Christ redeemed you at great price by His unjust death on the cross because He loves you beyond your human capacity to realize just now. Ask Mother Mary to help you accept her unconditional love for you as you pray for strong faith in God's unconditional, saving love for you. Trust that you have strong protection in the intercessory power of Saint Joseph. Be grateful that you are a vital member of the Holy Family of the Most Holy Trinity. Conclude by praying the prayer you have selected.

If you persevere with this prayerful, meditative exercise daily, amazing interior images will be conveyed to your intellect. Your soul will begin to heal, and your interior life will grow as quickly as your own personal commitment to this prayer exercise continues. With perseverance, the virtue of hope will germinate in your soul. As your interior intellectual imaging prayer experience matures, notice how the sweet buds of love begin to scent the path of your daily life. Allow yourself to cherish being a most beloved member of the Holy Family of the Most Holy Trinity. Praise and thank God for this merciful blessing.

With Mother Mary's guidance, befriend the higher parts of your conscious awareness. Heavenly inspiration is a divine invitation. At some point in this process, as your faith matures, you will know in a way that transcends your intellect that Mother Mary gives you to her Son Jesus Christ swaddled in her virtues and nurtured with her pure love. Harm shall not come to you or those whom you love for Jesus Christ is Savior of all we prodigal children of our Heavenly Father are permitted to love while on earth.

Ponder the words of Jesus Christ in Revelation 2:15: *Behold, I make all things new.* Enter into the tranquility of Christ's victory over all the distortions of the earth. Jesus Christ, the Perfect Son, sanctifies and enriches everyone and everything His Mother Mary gives Him for the glory of the Most Holy Trinity.

Protection of a strong, holy, loyal and deeply loving human father is a vital part of our daily spiritual growth. Father and Doctor of the Church Saint Bernardine of Sienna bequeathed us this Consecration Prayer to Saint Joseph.

> Beloved Saint Joseph, adopt me as thy child. Protect and guard my salvation. Watch over me day and night. Preserve me under your cloak from all occasions of sin and distress. Obtain for me from the Divine Christ Child whom you protected and raised so valiantly, godly purity of body, mind and soul. Obtain for me from Jesus Christ, Son of God and son of your wife Mary, whom you adopted in obedience to the Angel of the Lord, a spirit of sacrifice, humility, self-denial, loyal commitment and sibling relationship with Jesus Christ now and for all eternity. Bless my dedicated love for Holy Mary my

mother, and her Divine Child, Jesus my brother. Saint Joseph, walk with me during my time on earth, be with me at my death and stand with me before Jesus, my merciful Savior, at the Judgement. Amen.

Countless people throughout the world, of all nations, backgrounds and beliefs, pray some part of the following prayer every day.

### THE *TE DEUM LAUDAMUS*

We praise thee, O Mother of God: we acknowledge thee to be the Virgin Mary.

All the earth acknowledges thee as the only all holy daughter of the Father.

All the angels and archangels serve thee.

The cherubim and seraphim praise thee and continually cry:

Holy, Holy, Mary, Mother of God, and pure Virgin,

Heaven and earth are filled with the majesty of thy glory.

The glorious choir of the Apostles praise thee.

The admirable company of the Prophets praise thee.

The white-robed army of martyrs praise thee.

The whole army of Confessors praise thee.

The Holy Church throughout the world doth acknowledge thee

An Empress of infinite majesty,

And a worthy Mother of the only Begotten Son.

And an Immaculate Spouse of the Holy Spirit.

Thou, O most Holy Virgin, art a Queen of honor.

Thou art the chosen daughter of the Eternal Father.

In order that man may be saved, thou hast conceived the Son of God in thy womb.

By thee the old serpent was crushed, and Heaven was opened to the faithful.

Thou dost sit at the right hand of thy Son in the glory of the Father.

Thou art believed to be the reconciler of the future Judge.

Therefore, we pray thee, to come to the assistance of thy servants whom thy Son has redeemed with His precious blood.

Help them to be numbered with thy saints in glory everlasting.

O Mary, save thy children and bless those who honor thee.

Govern them and lift them up forever.

Day by day, O Mary, we magnify thee, and we praise thy name forever.

Vouchsafe, O Mary, this day and always keep us from grievous sins.

O Mary, take pity upon us: take pity upon us.

O Mary, in thee have I hoped. Let me never be
confounded. Amen.

*Saint Bonaventure (c. 1221-1274)*
*Doctor of the Church*

## PRAYER OF HUMILIY

Lovely Lady dressed in blue,
Teach me how to pray!
God was just your little Boy,
Tell me what to say!

Did you lift Him up sometimes,
Gently, on your knee?
Did you sing to Him the way
Mother does to me?

Did you hold His hand at night?
Did you ever try
Telling stories of the world?
O, and did he cry?

Do you really think He cares
If I tell Him things—
Little things that happen?
And do the Angels' wings
Make a noise? And

Can He hear me if I speak low?
Does He understand me now?
Tell me—for you know!

Lovely Lady dressed in blue,
Teach me how to pray!
God was just your little Boy,
And you know the way.

*Mary Dixon Thayer (c. 1950)*

## PRAYER FOR AWARENESS
## OF JESUS AMONG US

O Holy Virgin Mary, Immaculate Mother of Jesus
And our mother,
We humbly invoke you under the title of
Our Lady of the Most Blessed Sacrament
because you are the Mother of our Savior who
Lives in the Holy Eucharist.
From you He took the flesh and blood He feeds us
in the Sacred Host.
We invoke you under that title because the
Grace of the Holy Eucharist comes to us through you,
the channel through which God's graces reach us.
Finally, we call you Our Lady of the Most Blessed
  Sacrament

because you were the first to live the Eucharistic life.
Teach us to pray the Holy Mass as you did,
to receive Holy Communion worthily and
    frequently,
and to visit devotedly with Our Lord Jesus in the
    Blessed Sacrament.
Amen.

*John Cardinal Carberry, S.T.D.*
*Archbishop of Saint Louis 1968-1979*

In earlier times, it was not so commonly known that from all eternity, Mary was created in the mind of God pre-redeemed, a perfected woman through the merits of the God-man she would bear, totally pure, totally immaculate, the holy of holies in which the Eternal Word of God, Jesus the Christ, would find entrance for the purpose of redeeming all His prodigal children of the earth. In the divine Plan, All-Holy Mary, most blessed among women, is thrice holy: of the Father, of the Son, and of the Holy Spirit.

In 1917, Franciscan Saint Maximilian Kolbe, who was later martyred at Auschwitz on August 14, 1941, founded a worldwide evangelization movement known as the Militia of the Immaculata. Members commit to Christ through Mary by means of life consecration to Mother Mary and filial witness to their Baptismal vows. Popularly known as MI's, over three million members worldwide strive to honor a soul-piercing line in *Ineffabilis Deus* (1854 Papal Dogma of the Immaculate Conception of All-Holy Mary), "…it was quite fitting that, as the Only-begotten has a Father in Heaven, whom the Seraphim extol as trice-holy, so He should have a Mother on earth who would never be without the splendor of holiness."

MI's in modern times, especially among millennials who value freedom, flexibility and performance, strive for self-sanctity and the sanctity of others with Christ through Mary as their central purpose of life on earth. The MI motto is: "Lead every individual with Mother Mary to the Sacred Heart of Jesus Christ". The following prayer is from their Founder, Saint Maximilian Kolby.

## PRAYER OF PRAISE

Let me praise you, O most holy Virgin!
Let me praise you at my own cost.
Let me live, work, waste away and die, for you alone.
Let me contribute to your exaltation, to your highest
  exaltation.
Permit that others may outdo my zeal in glorifying
  you, O Mary,
so that by holy rivalry your glory may grow more
  rapidly,
just as He wills it, who raised you above all creatures.
In you alone, God has been more adored than in all
  other saints,

For you God created the world, and for you He
   created me also.
O let me praise you, most holy Virgin Mary.
   *Saint Maximilian Kolbe (c. 1894–1941)*

Sacred Tradition has taught us that the devotion of remember-
ing and honoring seven specific sorrows of Mary will restore
faith and hope to broken-hearts and ruined families. The *Seven
Sorrows of Mary* devotion miraculously brings divine sweetness
to human sorrow and is a means of repairing human destruc-
tion. The healing effect of this ancient, world-wide Marian
devotion draws heavenly strength, confidence in God's salvific
power, and commitment to the loving, tender help of Mother
Mary during our entire lifespan on earth.

## PRAYERS OF MARY'S SEVEN SORROWS

O God, come to my assistance.
O Lord make haste to help us.
Glory be to the Father, and to the Son, and to the
Holy Spirit,
As it was in the beginning, is now, and ever shall be,
Now and forever. Amen.

1. I grieve with you, O Mary most sorrowful, in the affliction of your tender heart at the prophecy of holy and aged Simeon and Anna when you presented your precious Infant Jesus in the Temple.

Dear Mother, by your Immaculate Heart so afflicted, obtain for me the virtue of humility and the gift of holy fear of God forever.

*(Pray the Our Father, Hail Mary, and Glory Be.)*

2. I grieve with you, O Mary most sorrowful, in the anguish of your most loving, immaculate heart, during your flight with your Infant Jesus and Saint Joseph into Egypt, and during your sojourn there.

Dear Mother, by your immaculate heart so troubled, obtain for me the virtue of generosity, especially toward the poor, and the gift of piety.

*(Pray the Our Father, Hail Mary, and Glory Be.)*

3. I grieve with you, O Mary most sorrowful, in those anxieties which tried your troubled immaculate heart at the loss of your dear Son Jesus for three days when He was an adolescent.

Dear Mother, by your immaculate heart so full of anguish, obtain for me the virtue of chastity and the gift of knowledge.

*(Pray the Our Father, Hail Mary, and Glory Be.)*

4. I grieve with you, O Mary most sorrowful, in the pain of your immaculate heart at meeting Jesus as He carried His cross.

Dear Mother, by your immaculate heart so troubled, obtain for me the virtue of patience and the gift of fortitude.

(*Pray the Our Father, Hail Mary, and Glory Be.*)

5. I grieve with you, O Mary most sorrowful, in the martyrdom which your generous immaculate heart endured as you stood near Jesus Christ during His crucifixion.

Dear Mother, by your afflicted immaculate heart, obtain for me the virtue of temperance and the gift of counsel.

(*Pray the Our Father, Hail Mary, and Glory Be.*)

6. I grieve with you, O Mary most sorrowful, in the wounding of your tender immaculate heart, when the side of Jesus Christ was struck by the lance before His body was removed from the cross.

Dear Mother, by your immaculate heart thus transfixed, obtain for me the virtue of fraternal charity and the gift of understanding.

*Pray the Our Father, Hail Mary, and Glory Be.*)

7. I grieve with you, O Mary most sorrowful, for the pangs that wrenched your most loving immaculate heart at the burial of Jesus Christ.

Dear Mother, by your immaculate heart, sunk in the bitterness of desolation, obtain for me the virtue of diligence and the gift of wisdom.

*(Pray the Our Father, Hail Mary, and Glory Be.)*

Let us pray.

May the intercession of Your Mother,

Whose most holy soul was pierced by a sword of sorrow in the hour of Your bitter passion, be made for us,

We beseech You, O Lord Jesus Christ,

Now and at the hour of our death, before the Throne of Your Mercy.

Through You, O Jesus Christ, Savior of the world, Who with the Father and the Holy Spirit

Lives and reigns world without end. Amen.

*Author unknown*

Here is a luminous excerpt from the Little Compline with the Akathist Hymn blessing Mary, Mother of God.

## THEOTOKOS

It is truly right to bless you, O Theotokos, who are
    ever
blessed and all-blameless, and the Mother of our God.
More honorable than the Cherubim, and more
    glorious
beyond compare than the Seraphim,
You who without stain bore God the Word,
Are truly Theotokos.
We magnify you.

I shall open my mouth and it will be filled with the
    Spirit,
and I shall speak forth to the Queen and Mother.
I shall be seen joyfully singing her praises,
and I shall delight to sing of her wonders.

Glory to the Father, and to the Son and to the Holy
    Spirit:
The ends of the earth do praise and bless you:
Hail, pure Maiden, Holy Scroll on which
The Finger of God did inscribe His Word.
Implore Him now, O Theotokos,
To write down your servants in the
Book of Life now and ever,
And unto ages of ages. Amen.

*Translated by the Very Reverend Joseph Rahal*

## THE MYSTICAL ROSE PRAYER

O virgin Mother, daughter of thy Son,
Created beings all in lowliness
Surpassing, as in height above them all,
Term by the eternal counsel pre-ordained,
Ennobler of thy nature, so advanced
In thee, that its great Maker did not scorn,
Himself, in His own work enclosed to dwell!
For in thy womb rekindling shone the love
Revealed, whose genial influence makes now
This flower to germinate in eternal peace!
Here thou to us, of charity and love,
Art, as the noon-day torch; and art, beneath,
To mortal men, of hope a living spring.
So mightily art thou, lady! and so great,
That he who grace desires, and comes not
To thee for aid, fain would have desire
Fly without wings. Nor only him who asks,
Thy bounty succors, but doth freely oft
Forerun the asking. Whatsoever may be
Of excellence in creature, pity mild,
Relenting mercy, large munificence,
All are combined in thee.

*Dante Alighieri (1265–1321)*

## PRAYER TO THE MOTHER OF GOD

At morn, at noon, at twilight dim—
Maria! thou have heard my hymn!
In joy and woe, in good and ill—
Mother of God, be with me still!

When the hours flew brightly by
And not a cloud obscured the sky,
My soul lest it should truant be,
Thy grace did guide to thine and thee.

Now, when storm of Fate o'ercast
Darkly my Present and my Past,
Let my future radiant shine,
With sweet hopes of thee and thine!

*Edgar Allan Poe (1809–1849)*

Those who cast no shadow roam the earth looking for Jesus the Christ. Everyone, everything needs Jesus Christ our Redeemer. Those who find His All-Holy Mother Mary discover the safest and quickest way to Jesus Christ.

## PRAYER TO MARY UNDOER OF KNOTS

O Virgin Mary, Faithful Mother who never refuses to help your children; Mother whose hands never cease to help because they are moved by the loving kindness of your Immaculate Heart; look upon me with compassion and undo the snarl of knots that exist in my life. You know all the pains and sorrows caused by these tangled knots. Mary, my Mother, I entrust to your loving hands the entire ribbon of my life. In your hands there is no knot that cannot be undone. Most Holy Mother pray for Divine Assistance to come to my aid. Take this knot (mention specific need) into your pure hands today. I beg you to undo this knot for the glory of God once and for all, in the Holy Name of your Son Jesus Christ. Amen.

*A favorite prayer of Pope Francis*

## PRAYER TO HEAVEN'S BRIGHT QUEEN

Let us soar away from this world's dominions,
And borrow awhile the meek turtle's pinions;
Let us mount to the home of the happy and blest,
Where the Saints and Angels eternally rest,

Nor tarry our flight on the borders of Heaven,
Since this privileged entrance by faith is given:
But on, still, still on, to the golden throne
Of God the Father, Who sits alone;
The Father, all present, omnipotent Being,
Almighty God, the great All-seeing.
Oh! to adore You, our Heavenly King
And forever and ever Your praises to sing!
But a mortal being must hasten on
Lest the light of faith should flee and be gone.
Lo! On the right is a glorious Throne
And another Who sits thereon alone,
The anointed Son of His Father's love,
Who ascended as God and man above.
But these mortal eyes must still veil Their sight
Nor glance at a Being so dazzling and bright.
How I long for the day when my soul shall adore
And gaze on these Beauties for evermore.
Near to the Throne of the Lamb that was slain
Sits His Mother, Queen of Heaven, Star of the main:
Her throne is of ivory, silver delight,
And with glittering pearls of the ocean is bright;
The diamond glows with the emerald's sheen
While the ruby and amethyst there are seen.
If such be the splendor of Mary's throne
Encircled by Angels, a peerless zone,
What must her own perfect beauty be?
Dazzling with glorified majesty?

Her robe is of azure with sapphires delight
Fringed round with a border of silvery light.
Her tunic is gleaming with cloth of gold,
While brilliants are glowing in every fold.
Her face which was ever too lovely for earth,
The Holy Spirit beautifies round her the while,
She repays all homage with humility's dear smile.
On that queenly head is a golden crown
Which presses the hair but gently down:
On its front is a star whose dazzling sheen
Befits the brow of God's beloved Queen,
While its rim is fringed with a wreath of roses
Sweeter than earth's fondest vision discloses.
Fifty are crimson, and fifty are blue,
And fifty again of the lily's hue.
The sun never shone on such flowers as those
Which might tempt one to wonder if earth hath its
    rose.
This Rosary hung on its chain of gold,
And I pondered thereon until reason told
How the Queen of the Saints from that Heaven's
    sphere
Looks down on the earth each petition to hear,
And by loved intercession the meek prayer to heed
Which her children upraise in their hour of need.

*Saint John Henry Cardinal Neuman (c. 1801–1890)*

## CHAPTER 9

# MOTHER OF CHRIST

## THE POWER OF
## THE HOLY ROSARY

The Holy Rosary, familiarly known as the spiritual chain that binds generations to eternal life, unleashes a loving torrent of divine mercy upon families, groups, cities and nations. A meditative prayer pilgrimage through the New Testament, the Rosary is composed of joyful, luminous, sorrowful, and glorious mysteries of the life of Jesus Christ, along with specific Rosary prayers. These reveal the way, truth and life of Jesus Christ on earth and in the afterlife in perfect harmony with our Heavenly Father's Plan. Everyone can benefit from that knowledge. The Holy Rosary mysteries and prayers illumine our divinely established path to the mountain of peace, God's Plan for all His prodigal children.[1]

At Lourdes in 1856 and again at Fatima in 1917, Mother Mary, whose loving kindness never fails us, asked all people to pray the Holy Rosary. Marian apparitions requesting return to the Holy Rosary continue throughout the world. People from all walks of life and faith traditions have responded.[2] Immense graces flow from the Holy Rosary and life is happier as we learn its lessons.[3]

Death is not the last chapter in our personal book of life. In the interim between Mother Mary's apparitions at Lourdes and Fatima, on September 8, 1893, Pope Leo XIII wrote an encyclical entitled *Laetitiae Sanctae* about some of the extraordinary, highly desirable graces flowing from the Holy Rosary. This encyclical identifies three pernicious tendencies at work to bring society and each of us to degradation, denigration, despair, and eternal death. They are distaste for a simple life with fulfillment through sanctified labor, abhorrence of suffering of any kind, and forgetfulness of a future life.

*Laetitiae Sanctae* points out practical solutions for the world's ailments that we discover in the prayers and meditations of the Holy Rosary. Only the foolhardy would disregard such an effective spiritual safety net.[4]

## THE LEGACY OF SAINT DOMINIC

Saint Dominic (c. 1170-1221), born into a patrician family in Castile, Spain, was attracted to the blessings flowing within prayer, fasting and almsgiving from early childhood. This spiritual discipline provided clarity of thought and a degree of peace that insulated him from the misery he recognized in those trapped in relentless demands of passing pleasures, maintenance of power, or worldly wealth.

Solitude was a highly valued treasure for young Dominic. The boy grew into a refined man relentlessly pursuing the numinous mystery of God's omnipresence.

Dominic was ordained a Roman Catholic priest at the age of twenty-four. He intuited eternal happiness hidden in ordinariness and chose a life of solitude in a monastery. Because he personally experienced God's scorching love, Dominic felt compelled to look for ways to reciprocate that indefinable, unconditional love of our Heavenly Father for each of His dearly redeemed prodigal children. But what can a mere human give to Divine Omnipotence?

Grace flooded Dominic's soul with consciousness of our Heavenly Father pining for the reciprocal love of his prodigal children of the earth. Burning with zeal to awaken human souls to God's immense, unfathomable love for each of us, Dominic accompanied his Bishop on a missionary tour in France. The raging fire of love for Christ in Dominic's heart was so intense that it fanned dying embers in souls who came in contact with him. Because he was able to communicate Gospel truth with simplicity that melted icy hearts, his reputation and missionary projects grew.

Gradually, fervent men joined Dominic. This group became known as the Order of Preachers (Dominicans), a mendicant religious order, now worldwide, whose mission is to preach the good news of the Holy Gospel of Jesus Christ to all our Heavenly Father's prodigal children of the earth.

Academic proficiency, penance, prayer and asceticism for the glory of God enabled early Dominicans to penetrate scriptural mysteries. Saint Albert the Great, a numinous mystic and the foremost intellectual of his times is also known as Albertus Magnus.[5] He and his star pupil, Saint Thomas Aquinas, are brilliant medieval Dominican luminaries and Doctors of the Church who are highly revered and respected throughout the modern world.

Humble founder Saint Dominic recognized that our sins (bad choices) weigh us down and blind us to God's unconditionally loving, providential omnipresence. Unimaginable tragedy flows from that disfunction. Inspired by the Holy Spirit, Dominic prayerfully opened the Scriptures for seekers to help them become aware of hidden treasures within their own souls that are accessed through the sacraments. Dominic's self-effacing simplicity, thoroughly infused with divine light, enabled sincere people to successfully assume responsibility for their personal gifts and eternal destiny in harmony with gospel truths.

Saint Dominic was a supernaturally effective preacher and mysteriously gifted theologian. History tells us he raised the dead, healed the sick and restored the brokenhearted. He never tired of explaining that every human soul on earth, consciously or unconsciously, needs Jesus Christ, the Word of God made flesh in the womb of immaculate Mary, His thrice holy Virgin Mother of Nazareth.[6]

More and more people recognized the heavenly luminosity of the Living God that encapsulated Saint Dominic. He was a beacon beaming on the largely unrecognized opportunity for eternal bliss enclosed within each human soul that is actualized by unrestricted faith in Jesus Christ.

History identifies Saint Dominic as a mystic warrior defending the truths of the Holy Gospel. He met Saint Francis of Assisi in a dream and later in Rome in person.[7] These two remarkable Christian men of history shared the common goal of union with God through total commitment to His divine Plan revealed in the Holy Gospel. Through the centuries, Dominicans and Franciscans have continuously striven to honor their Founders' strategic encounter with mutual friendship.

At twilight of the High Middle Ages, worship of a golden calf consisting of power, wealth, luxury, ease and prestige emerged like a tidal wave, drowning in its wake faith in God's providential love for His prodigal children. As fewer and fewer recognized or cared about the good news of the Holy Gospel, the Furies stirred their pots and unrest broke out everywhere.

Generationally handed-down history speaks of deeply distressed Saint Dominic withdrawing into a dense forest to fast and pray for divine guidance amid the corrupt culture of materialism. He was keenly aware of the suffering that godlessness brings to the psyche, body, soul, and spirit of people who forfeit Gospel truths for an immediate bowl of poison porridge.

Dominic perceived piercing cries of soon-to-be perpetually starved prodigal children rushing headlong into the Dungeons of the Damned. Materialism's infectious potions contaminated the purity of their innermost being and they were unable to tolerate Divine Truth revealed in the Holy Gospel.

Godlessness flows from unrecognized sins of people of all times who export and bequeath their contaminated behavior. Such soot-soaked souls cannot find the mountain of peace. They wander aimlessly through the Valleys of Death seeking relief from death's rotten claws that cling to them. Compliance with Divine Truth illuminated within the Holy Gospel of Jesus Christ washes people of eternal death.[8] Divine Truth unleashes redeeming grace, the antidote to the poison of widespread compromise with the Holy Gospel.[9]

In the Spirit, Dominic saw the poorest of the poor— those who do not know the tender, life-giving, healing love of Jesus Christ. The enormity of their heinous, self-chosen fate overwhelmed Saint Dominic. Aware that he was but a small, weak instrument in God's mighty hands, this faithful, ordained servant of Christ prayerfully pleaded for massive infusions of Christ's redemptive grace to advance the Kingdom of our Heavenly Father on earth. Uniting himself deeply in prayer with Christ Crucified, Dominic collapsed upon the hardened, sin-stained ground. His bloody tears of atonement soaked the dying earth.

Overshadowed by a mysterious, grace-filled cloud of mercy, Dominic discerned the loving presence of Mother Mary nearby. History recounts little of that event. It is recorded however in the saga of Dominican annals that Christ's Heaven-sent Mother was accompanied by three luminescent, powerfully protective angels.

Dominic was aware that each lost soul pierces Mary's heart anew. Supernatural zeal steeped in the sacrificial love of Jesus Christ for suffering sinners invigorated Saint Dominic: if even one soul finds Divine Truth within the Holy Gospel, it is worth best efforts in all times and places.

Mother Mary presented a celestial remedy from Jesus Christ for suffering souls of all generations to Saint Dominic.

> "My Son Jesus gives you a weapon from the Divine Trinity to reform the world. The Incarnation of Jesus Christ is the foundation stone of the New Testament. In this kind of spiritual warfare, wherein God's people are enslaved to cravings of their earth-crusted appetites and have lost sight of Divine Truth, the battering ram is the Angelic Psalter. Immortal souls trapped in shrouded earth allures are won over to God through supernatural graces of the Holy Rosary."

Thereafter, angels only Saint Dominic could see rang the great cathedral bells to summon people when he preached about the numinous graces of the Holy Rosary. Mystical phenomena continued to surround Saint Dominic as he preached the wonders of the Holy Rosary, so much so that graces of the Holy Rosary continue to fall like manna from heaven upon spiritually sick, starving souls all over the earth.

For centuries, our Christian ancestors have entered into the sunlight of Sacred Truth contained in the Holy Rosary. Jesus the Christ reveals Himself through the mysteries, meditations and prayers of the Holy Rosary.[10] He warns us, *"Amen I say to you, unless you be converted, and become as little children, you shall not enter into the kingdom of heaven".*[11]

At twilight of the twentieth century, a reasonably humble layman remarked offhandedly: "Every *Hail Mary* prayer in the Rosary works like a jack hammer on the thick crust of generational bondage encasing our souls. Respect the Rosary. We all need it."

Not surprisingly, where the Holy Rosary is faithfully prayed, divine grace draws down divine protection. Pope Saint Paul VI stressed the element of contemplation within the prayer of the Holy Rosary, in addition to its value of praise and petition. He warned that without contemplation during the Holy Rosary, it becomes "a body without a soul, and its recitation is in danger of becoming a mechanical repetition of formulas".

For many centuries our Christian ancestors have held fast to the belief that the Holy Rosary, prayed properly, is indeed the chain that binds generations to eternal life. But there is more. Now we know there are immediate, health-related benefits derived from the Holy Rosary. Eminent physician Dr. Luciano Bernardi reported in the *British Medical Journal* that praying the Holy Rosary, especially in Latin, among other effects, synchronizes all the heart rhythms.[12] Our immortal souls animate our bodies.[13]

Four hundred years ago, Saint Louis de Montfort discovered at least seven spiritual effects within souls who faithfully pray the Holy Rosary.[14] These include but are not limited to gradual acquisition of knowledge of Jesus the Christ, soul purification, victory over enemies, facility in the practice of virtue, reverent loyalty to Jesus Christ, material and spiritual means to fulfill obligations to God and neighbor, supernatural graces and merits. [15]

Faith assures us that our Heavenly Father unconditionally loves us and desires the best for us. He created us to share His infinite happiness. That is His perfect Plan for us. Unfortunately, most of us don't know how to follow our Heavenly Father's individual, unique Plan for our life on earth and ever after. When we make mistakes, our Heavenly Father anguishes over our poor choices and their painful consequences for us and those we love. Long ago, He sent His only begotten Son Jesus Christ to earth through Mary to save us from our bondage to such misery.

Christ's entire life on earth was perfect conformity to our Heavenly Father's Plan. Tenderness and kindness drove all His actions, even to confrontations with the scribes and pharisees. When He turned the tables of the money changers in the Temple, Christ's colleagues were astounded at the kindness of His ways. No loss inured to anyone, yet He made His point. Those who witnessed His execution were astonished at His love and patience and acceptance, not only of our Heavenly Father's Plan for Him, but of the limitations of those who inflicted punishment upon Him. In His sacred innocence, Jesus Christ brought joy and peace, even to those who wished Him ill.

Jesus Christ gave us His own most faithful, highly tested mother Mary to help us bond with Him every moment of our sojourn on earth.[16] Each lost soul slashes Mother Mary's heart. With technology prevalent throughout the world, scarcity of Divine Truth cries out to every faithful follower of Christ for remediation. The vineyard is overripe. Souls are dying for want of the Holy Gospel. Christ calls through Mary for action.[17]

Mother Mary humbly and quietly invites all her Son's humble followers to become her little children. She encourages her children to sing to her most humble Infant, praise Him, give Him hospitality in their hearts and homes, and courageously follow Him to the Heights of the Mountain of Peace. Along the way, Mother Mary teaches her dear little children to breathe divine air of joy and peace; heal their sin-wounded souls on purity of thought, word, and deed. Mother Mary faithfully cares for all her cherished children who are forever Christ's younger brothers and sisters.[18] In every generation, Mother Mary tenderly holds each one close in her immaculate heart as they learn to wash themselves of clinging claws of death that rot the fibers of their souls. Mother Mary gently, softly and silently helps them grow into children of Eternal Life.[19]

The Lord Jesus Christ is the Divine Physician.[20] He is readily available to His Mother's children. Mother Mary soothingly protects her little ones who accept Christ's supernatural vaccine of sacramental Baptism. She carefully tends her beloved children who accept His sacramental booster vaccines of Confirmation, Reconciliation, Holy Eucharist, Holy Matrimony, Holy Orders and finally His sacrament of Holy Anointing of the Sick and Dying.

Though we cling to the whistling mane of every wind like all who flee Christ's saving love, we are children of Mary because He gave us to His Mother, Our Lady of Golgotha. Christ the Eternal Highpriest welcomes His Mother's children into His Sacred Heart. In the Sacred Heart of Jesus, Mary's children dwell in the depths of the Most Holy Trinity. With Christ through Mary on the peaks of the mountain of peace, our Heavenly Father's redeemed prodigal children soar to His outstretched arms in the Heavenly Kingdom prepared for them from the foundation of the world.[21]

## PRAYER STRUCTURE OF THE HOLY ROSARY

The Holy Rosary is prayed by holding a rosary, which is a string of beads designed to accommodate each of the prayers. A crucifix and a medal are attached to the string of beads. A rosary can be made of the most exquisite gems or of the simplest beads. If rosary beads are unavailable, ten fingers can serve as markers for the prayers of the Holy Rosary. As a person says a prayer of the Holy Rosary or meditates upon a Scriptural scene, he or she holds the bead designated for that particular part of the Holy Rosary. The bead serves as a point of meditation, a reminder to keep one's mind focused on the prayer-filled pilgrimage through the New Testament.

The Holy Rosary is divided into the Joyful, Luminous, Sorrowful, and Glorious Mysteries of the Life of Christ. Each mystery is made up of five decades, and each decade consists of one Our Father, ten Hail Marys, a Glory Be to the Father, and the Jesus Mercy prayer. The prayers and mysteries follow.

First, with the crucifix of the Rosary Beads, make the *Sign of the Cross*. Still holding the crucifix, pray the *Apostles' Creed*. A large bead follows the crucifix, and after that is a series of three small beads and then another large one. Pray one *Our Father Prayer* on the large bead, a *Hail Mary Prayer* on each of the three small beads, and a *Glory Be to the Father Prayer* on the large bead. At this point, you will have reached the medal.

Now, holding the medal, start the First Joyful Mystery by meditating on the Scriptural scene. Then, on the same medal, pray the *Our Father Prayer*. Ten small beads will follow the medal, and then a large bead. (This series of ten beads plus a large bead is called a decade, and there are five decades on Rosary Beads.) Pray a *Hail Mary Prayer* on each of the ten small beads, and on the large bead pray the *Glory Be to the Father Prayer*, along with the *Jesus Mercy Prayer*. Start the Second Joyful Mystery on the same large bead and continue this pattern until you have reached the end of the Fifth Joyful Mystery and have once again returned to the medal. Conclude by praying the *Hail, Holy Queen Prayer*.

If desired, repeat the Holy Rosary pattern with the Luminous, Sorrowful and Glorious Mysteries. Some people pray the entire four Mysteries of the Holy Rosary every day. Others prefer to pray only one Mystery per day. Many like to follow this pattern each week:

| | |
|---|---|
| Sunday: | The Glorious Mystery |
| Monday: | The Joyful Mystery |
| Tuesday: | The Sorrowful Mystery |
| Wednesday: | The Glorious Mystery |
| Thursday: | The Joyful Mystery |
| Friday: | The Sorrowful Mystery |
| Saturday: | The Luminous Mystery |

## THE PRAYERS OF THE HOLY ROSARY

### THE SIGN OF THE CROSS

In the name of the Father and the Son
and the Holy Spirit. Amen.

### THE APOSTLES' CREED

I believe in God, the Father Almighty, Creator of
Heaven and earth, and in Jesus Christ, His only Son,

Our Lord, who was conceived by the Holy Spirit, born of the Virgin Mary, suffered under Pontius Pilate, was crucified, died, and was buried. He descended to the dead; the third day, He rose again; He ascended into Heaven, and is seated at the right Hand of God, the Father Almighty; from thence He shall come to judge the living and the dead. I believe in the Holy Spirit, the Holy Catholic Church, the Communion of Saints, the forgiveness of sins, the resurrection of the body, and life everlasting. Amen.

### THE OUR FATHER PRAYER

Our Father Who art in Heaven, hallowed be Thy Name, Thy Kingdom come, Thy will be done on earth as it is in Heaven. Give us this day our daily bread and forgive us our trespasses as we forgive those who trespass against us, and lead us not into temptation, but deliver us from evil. Amen.

### THE HAIL MARY PRAYER

Hail Mary, full of grace, the Lord is with thee. Blessed art thou amongst women and blessed is the fruit of thy womb, Jesus. Holy Mary, Mother of God, pray for us sinners, now and at the hour of our death. Amen.

### THE GLORY BE TO THE FATHER PRAYER

Glory be to the Father, and to the Son, and to the Holy Spirit, as it was in the beginning, is now and ever shall be, world without end. Amen.

### THE JESUS MERCY PRAYER

O my Jesus, forgive us our sins, save us from the fires of hell. Lead all souls to Heaven, especially those who have most need of Thy Mercy. Amen.

### THE HAIL, HOLY QUEEN PRAYER

Hail, holy Queen, Mother of Mercy. Hail our life, our sweetness and our hope. To thee do we cry, poor banished children of Eve; to thee do we send up our sighs, mourning, and weeping in this vale of tears. Turn then, most gracious Advocate, thine eyes of mercy towards us, and after this, our exile, show us the blessed fruit of thy womb, Jesus; O clement, O loving, O sweet Virgin Mary. Pray for us, O holy Mother of God, that we may be made worthy of the promises of Christ, thy Son. Amen.

## THE JOYFUL MYSTERIES
## OF THE HOLY ROSARY

The first five decades, the Joyful Mysteries of the Holy Rosary, focus on five joyful Scriptural events in the life of Jesus Christ. They are divided into five joyful scenes from the Bible.

*The First Joyful Mystery: The Annunciation (Luke 1:26–38)*
The angel said to her, "Mary, do not be afraid; you have won God's favor. Listen! You are to conceive and bear a Son and you must name Him Jesus."

*The Second Joyful Mystery: The Visitation (Luke 1:39–45)*
And Elizabeth was filled with the Holy Spirit and cried out with a loud voice, saying, "Blessed art thou among women and blessed is the fruit of thy womb."

*The Third Joyful Mystery: The Nativity (Luke 2:1–7)*
And she brought forth her firstborn Son and wrapped Him in swaddling clothes and laid Him in a manger, because there was no room for them in the inn.

*The Fourth Joyful Mystery: The Presentation (Luke 2:22–39)*
And when the days of her purification were fulfilled according to the Law of Moses, they took Him up to Jerusalem to present Him to the Lord.

*The Fifth Joyful Mystery: The Finding of the Child Jesus in the Temple (Luke 2:41–52)*
And it came to pass after three days, that they found Him in the temple, sitting in the midst of the teachers, both listening to them and asking them questions.

## THE LUMINOUS MYSTERIES
## OF THE HOLY ROSARY

The second five decades, the Luminous Mysteries of the Holy Rosary, illumine the public ministry of Jesus. They are divided into five luminous scriptural scenes in the New Testament.

*The First Luminous Mystery: Jesus' Baptism in the Jordan (Matthew 3:13)*
Then Jesus came from Galilee to John at the Jordan to be baptized.

*The Second Luminous Mystery: Jesus' Self Revelation at the Wedding Feast of Cana (John 2:11)*

Jesus did this (turned water into wine) at the beginning of his signs in Cana in Galilee and so revealed his glory, and his disciples began to believe in him.

*The Third Luminous Mystery: Jesus' Proclamation of the Kingdom (Mark 1:14-15)*
After John had been arrested, Jesus came to Galilee proclaiming the Gospel of God: "This I the time of fulfillment. The kingdom of God is at hand. Repent, and believe in the gospel."

*The Fourth Luminous Mystery: Jesus' Transfiguration (Luke 9:28, 29)*
He took Peter, John, and James and went up the mountain to pray. While he was praying, Moses and Elijah appeared with him and his face changed in appearance and his clothing became dazzling white.

*The Fifth Luminous Mystery: Jesus Institutes the Holy Eucharist (Mark 14:22-24)*
While they were eating, he took bread, said the blessing, broke it, and gave it to them, and said, 'Take it; this is my body.' Then he took a cup, gave thanks, and gave it to them, and they all drank from it. He said to them, 'This is my blood of the covenant, which will be shed for many.'"

# THE SORROWFUL MYSTERIES
## OF THE HOLY ROSARY

The third five decades, the Sorrowful Mysteries of the Holy Rosary, illumine the passion and death of Jesus. They are divided into five sorrowful scriptural scenes in the New Testament.

*The First Sorrowful Mystery: Christ's Agony in the Garden (Luke 22:44)*
And being in an agony he prayed more earnestly; and his sweat became like great drops of blood falling down upon the ground.

*The Second Sorrowful Mystery: Christ's Scourging at the Pillar (John 19:1)*
Then Pilate took Jesus and had him scourged.

*The Third Sorrowful Mystery: Christ's Crowning with Thornes (Matthew 27:28-30)*
They stripped him and put a scarlet robe on him, and then twisted together a crown of thorns and set it on his head…They spit on him and took the staff and struck him on the head again and again.

*The Fourth Sorrowful Mystery: Christ Carries His Cross (John 19:17)*
Carrying his own cross, he went out to the place of the Skull, (which in Aramaic is called Golgotha).

*The Fifth Sorrowful Mystery: Christ's Crucifixion and Death (Luke 23:33-46)*

When they came to the place called the Skull, they crucified him there…. Jesus called out with a loud voice, "Father, into your hands I commit my spirit". When he had said this, he breathed his last.

## THE GLORIOUS MYSTERIES
## OF THE HOLY ROSARY

The fourth five decades, the Glorious Mysteries of the Holy Rosary, illumine the glorious scriptural mysteries of Jesus. They are divided into five glorious scriptural scenes in the New Testament.

*The First Glorious Mystery: Christ's Resurrection from the Dead (Luke 24: 1-49*

…They found the stone rolled away from the tomb, but when they entered, they did not find the body of Jesus…suddenly two men in clothes that gleamed like lightening stood beside them….and said…. "He is not here, he has risen"

*The Second Glorious Mystery: Christ's Ascension into Heaven (Luke 24:50)*

…Lifting up His hands, he blessed them. While he

was blessing them, he withdrew from them and was carried up into heaven.

*The Third Glorious Mystery: The Descent of the Holy Spirit (Acts 2:4)*
And they were all filled with the Holly Spirit and began to peak in different tongues, as the Spirit enabled them to proclaim.

*The Fourth Glorious Mystery: The Assumption of Mary (Rev. 12:1; Song of Songs 2:10, 11, 14; Psalm 45:13, 14; Jth. 15:10)*
A great sign appeared in the sky, a woman clothed with the sun....

*The Fifth Glorious Mystery: The Coronation of Mary (Judith 15:10–11; Song of Songs 1:1; 6:10; Ecclus. 24:4–9; Prov. 8:32–35;)*
Thou art the glory of Jerusalem, thou art the joy of Israel, thou art the honour of our people. . .. the hand of the Lord hath strengthened thee, and therefore thou shalt be blessed forever.

## THE DIVINE PROMISES
## OF THE HOLY ROSARY

Jesus Christ sent His Mother Mary to Saint Dominic with fifteen Promises for everyone who faithfully prays the Holy Rosary. Treasure the mysteries of the Holy Rosary, ponder them from generation to generation and reap their promises for all eternity.

1. To all those who pray the Holy Rosary devotedly, I promise my special protection and immense graces.

2. Those who will persevere in praying the Holy Rosary shall receive some signal grace.

3. Praying the Holy Rosary shall be a most powerful armor against hell; it shall destroy vice, deliver from sin, and shall dispel heresy.

4. Praying the Holy Rosary shall make virtue and good works flourish and shall obtain for souls the most abundant divine mercies; it shall substitute in hearts love of God for love of the world, elevate them to desire heavenly and eternal goods.

5. Those who entrust themselves to me through the Holy Rosary shall not perish.

6. Those who pray the Holy Rosary, fervently, meditating on its Mysteries, shall not be overwhelmed by misfortune, nor die a bad death. The sinner shall be converted; the just shall grow in grace

and become worthy of eternal life.

7. Those truly devoted to the Holy Rosary shall not die without the consolations of the Church, or without grace.

8. Those who pray the Holy Rosary shall find during their life and at their death the Light of God, the fullness of God's grace, and shall share in the merits of the blessed.

9. I will deliver very promptly from Purgatory the souls devoted to the Holy Rosary.

10. The true children of the Holy Rosary shall enjoy great glory in heaven.

11. What you ask through the Holy Rosary you shall obtain.

12. Those who make known the graces of the Holy Rosary shall obtain aid in all their necessities.

13. All the children of the Holy Rosary shall have for their friends and confidants in life and death the saints of heaven.

14. Those who pray the Holy Rosary faithfully are my beloved children, the brothers and sisters of Jesus Christ.

15. Devotion to the Holy Rosary is a special sign of predestination.

*Imprimatur*
*Patrick J. Hayes, D.D.*
*Archbishop of New York, 1919-1938*

# AUTHOR'S NOTE

Saint Theresa of Calcutta founded the Missionaries of Charity to spread the kingdom of the immaculate heart of Mary among the poorest of the poor. Over the centuries, it is clearer that the poorest of the poor are those who do not know Mary's Son Jesus the Christ. Saint Theresa of Calcutta challenged everyone to remember that we can never be all in for Jesus Christ if our love for His Blessed Mother Mary is not a living reality. Her directive: *Come close to Mary that she can take you to Jesus Christ. Avoid many distractions. Be alone with Jesus and ask His Mother Mary over and over again "Make me only all in for Jesus Christ"*[1]

The origin of this work belongs to Saint Theresa of Calcutta. She told the author: *The Blessed Mother wants me to write a prayer for your next book.* CHRIST THROUGH MARY flows from the singularity of that clarion call at dusk of the twentieth century.

PRAYER TO BE ALL IN FOR JESUS CHRIST

Mary, Mother of Jesus
Help me to be only
All for Jesus
Holy[2]

*Saint Theresa of Calcutta*

# ACKNOWLEDGEMENTS

Pope Saint John Paul II and Bishop Roman Danylak graciously consecrated this work to the Most Holy Trinity during their concelebrated Mass together at the Vatican on November 24, 1995.

Robert Faricy, S.J., S.T.D, Rev. Professor of Mystical Theology at Pontifical Gregorian University graciously wrote the Foreword to this work.

The text of this work was edited in Rome at Gregorian University under the direction of Rev. Professor Robert Faricy, S.J. and contains a distilled collection of significant prayers, insights and quotations from Doctors of the Church, Saints, Popes, Notables, Liturgies and Councils from the documents of history. Language from antiquity is slightly adapted in conformity with modern linguistic usage.

The graciously rendered expertise of Rev. T.A. Thompson, S.M. and his colleagues at the International Marian Research Institute is herein reflected.

The Marian theological proficiency of Rev. Professor René Laurentin guided segments of this work.

Some prayers are used with the gracious permission of the SMOM British Association; Ravengate Press Publishers; Congregation of Marians of the Immaculate Conception; Antiochian Orthodox Christian Archdiocese of North America.

Countless followers of Jesus Christ from around the world graciously helped to bring this book to life.

Multitudes of kind Children of Mary who humbly desire to remain anonymous graciously participated in this work

The author's spouse, children, grandchildren, great grandchild, spiritual children, colleagues and readers sacrificially provided love, inspiration and encouragement which are the foundation for this work.

May the Lord bless, protect and keep us all in the Palm of His Hand forever.

# NOTES

## INTRODUCTION

1  Luke 15:11-32
2  Genesis 3:15; Isaiah 7:14
3  Luke 1:38
4  John 1:12
5  Luke 1:32-38; Matthew 1:21-23
6  John 1:12-14; 17:21, 19:26-27; Genesis 3:15
7  Exodus 20:12
8  John 2:5
9  Genesis 3:15; Luke 1:26-28; John 19:26
10  Luke 1:38; John 1:14; 1 John 4:7-8
11  11John 17:21
12  Luke 2:46-51
13  John 2:3-5
14  Revelation 3:22
15  Matthew 7:7
16  Matthew 17:1-8; Mark 9:2-8; Luke 9:28-36; John 1:14; 2 Peter 1-16-18
17  Ezekiel 36:26
18  Romans 8:10; 2 Corinthians 4:6-7; Galatians 1:15-16, 2:20, 4:19; Ephesians 3:17; Colossians 1:27; 2 Thessalonians 1:10
19  John 16:33
20  Revelation 12:1

[21] Luke 2:35

[22] John 1:16

[23] Philippians 4:7

[24] John 2:3

[25] Matthew 19:19

[26] Matthew 6:5-6

[27] John 14:2

[28] Psalms 59:9, 69:28; Daniel 12:1; Malachi 3:16; Luke 10:20; Hebrews 12:23; Philippians 4:3; Revelation 3:5, 13:8, 17:8, 20:12, 15, 21:27, 22:19

[29] John 14:2

[30] Matthew 2:9-11

[31] John 16:24

[32] Matthew 7:7-8

[33] 2 Corinthians 9:6-8

[34] 2 Corinthians 12:9

[35] John 3:16-18

[36] Luke 1:43-44; Matthew 2:1-12

[37] John 19:25-27; Acts 1:12-14

## CHAPTER 1

[1] John: 4:7

[2] Matthew 1:20

[3] Luke 1:44

[4] Acts 1:14

[5] There are 36 Doctors of the Church in the Latin Rite. Their

title indicates that these saints are known for eminent learning, a high degree of sanctity and by proclamation of the church. Furthermore, they have made significant contributions to the understanding and interpretation of sacred scripture and the development of church doctrine.

6 Julian Allason, ed., *Prayers of the Sovereign Military and Hospitaller Order of Malta* (London: Sovereign Military Order of Malta, British Association, 1989), p. 45.

7 From Lope de Vega, as quoted in William A. Walsh, ed., *Heavens Bright Queen* (New York: Carey-Stafford, 1906), p. 84.

## CHAPTER 2

1 Doctor of the Church Saint Theresa of Avila's *Interior Castle* is a brilliant resource regarding the interior kingdom of the human soul.

2 John 1:1-5

3 Luke 1:41-44

4 Luke 1:43

5 Luke 1:46-55

6 Professor Scott Hahn's book *Hail, Holy Queen: The Mother of God in the Word of God*, is a noble resource in this area.

7 Suzanne Noffke, O.P., ed., *The Prayers of Catherine of Siena* (New York: Paulist Press, 1993), pp. 157–65, selected excerpts, provided through the graciousness of Rev. Professor Thomas M. King, S.J., S.T.D., Department of Theology, Georgetown University.

## CHAPTER 3

[1] John 2:11

[2] *Nihil obstat:* Jerome Curtin, D.C.L.; *Imprimi protest:* Kevin McNamara, Archbishop of Dublin, December 12, 1985.

[3] From the Basilica of the National Shrine of the Assumption of the Blessed Virgin Mary, Baltimore, Maryland.

[4] From a prayer card circulated in the crypt of the Basilica Shrine of the Immaculate Conception in Washington, DC.

## CHAPTER 4

[1] Matthew 18:20

[2] Luke 23:43

[3] Author interviews with eminent Marian theologian Rev. Professor René Laurentin.

[4] Ibid

[5] Ibid.

[6] John 14:21

[7] John 20:21

[8] Luke 12:36, 40

## CHAPTER 5

[1] Genesis 1:27; Wisdom 2:23

[2] John 3:16, 15:11

[3] Matthew 5:48

[4] Mark 10:18, Matthew 19:17; John 14:6

[5] John 14:6

[6] John14:15-31; 1Corinthians 1:24, 2:7; Colossians 1:26, 2:3, 3:3; Romans 11:33; Proverbs 8:24; Wisdom 10-16

[7] Luke 1:35; John 1:32-34, 14:26

[8] John 1:27

[9] 1 John 4:7-8; John 1:29

[10] Matthew 7:1-5

[11] Luke 1:38; John 1:14

[12] Anthony M. Buono, *Favorite Prayers to Our Lady* (New York: Catholic Book Publishing, 1991), p. 71.

[13] Saint M. Faustina Kowalska, *The Diary of Sister M. Faustina Kowalska, Divine Mercy in My Soul* (Stockbridge, MA: Marian Press, 1987), pp. 89–90, n. 161.

## CHAPTER 6

[1] Author interviews with eminent mystical theologian Rev. Professor Robert Faricy, S.J., S.T.D.

[2] The writings of Doctor of the Church Saint John of the Cross, especially *The Ascent of Mount Carmel,* explain the process.

[3.] Luke 1:26-38

[4.] *Imprimatur:* Patrick Cardinal Hayes, Archbishop of New York, September 5, 1936.

[5] Author unknown. Text of prayer from F. X. Lasance, *With God* (New York: Benziger Bros., 1911), pp. 720–23.

## CHAPTER 7

[1] Revelation 2:15

[2] *Regina Coeli* Prayer proper to the Easter liturgical season.

[3] *Ave Regina Coelorum tr.* Roman Hymnal, 1884. Slightly adapted.

[4] Buono, *Favorite Prayers to Our Lady, op. cit., p.* 73.

[5] Matthew J. O'Connell, ed., *The Imitation of Mary* (New York: Catholic Book Publishing, 1977), pp. 193–194.

[6] Adapted from *Prayers to Our Lady of Lourdes,* from approved sources. National Shrine of Our Lady of Lourdes, through the courtesy of Rev. Msgr. Hugh J. Phillips, Chaplain of the Grotto, Mount Saint Mary's College, Emmitsburg, MD.

[7] See my book *The Secrets of Mary* (New York: Saint Martin's Press, 2009), pp. 13-21.

[8] Ibid. pp. 177-186.

## CHAPTER 8

[1] Matthew 1:20

[2] Blessed William Chaminade as quoted by Rev. Donald H. Calloway, MIC, *Consecration to Saint Joseph* (Stockbridge, MA: Marian Fathers of the Immaculate Conception of the BVM, 2020), p. 14, referencing Saint Peter Julian Eymard, Endnote 1 in Part 1, p. 289.

## CHAPTER 9

[1] Rev. Dr. John A. Sanford, in his book *Mystical Christianity,* (New York: Crossroad Publishing Company, 1993), p. 300 alludes to God's Plan: ". . . the idea of Christianity is that God's work among us is a process begun by Christ and completed in the deification of the human soul and

the ultimate completion of the entire cosmos." Rev. Dr. Sanford refers to the vision of the Gospel of Saint John as ". . . one vast cosmic plan, which has existed from the beginning in the Mind of God, which is played out in the drama of what we call history, and in which each individual plays his or her small part."

[2] Janice T. Connell, *Meetings with Mary (New York: Ballantine Books, 1995)* and *The Visions of the Children (New York: St. Martin's Press, 1992, 1997, 2007).*

[3] Pope Saint John Paul II, Apostolic Letter *Rosarium Virginis Mariae* issued on October 16, 2002.

[4] In May 2021, Pope Francis called for global renewal of dedication to the Most Holy Rosary in order to be immersed in the sacred truth of the Holy Gospel.

[5] See my book *Prayer* Power (New York: HarperCollins Publishers,1998), pp. 5-15.

[6] Thrice Holy Virgin Mary is daughter of the Eternal Father, Mother of God the Son, Spouse of the Holy Spirit.

[7] See Endnote 5, pp. 46-58.

[8] 1 John 5:6

[9] Romans 5:8

[10] Matthew 18:3

[11] Pope Saint John Paul II called the faithful to "contemplate with Mary the face of Christ" in his Apostolic Letter *Rosarium Virginis Mariae.*

[12] Luciano Bernadi, *et al, British Medical Journal,* 2001; 323:1446-1449.

[13] See the seminal work in this area of research by Rev.

Professor Robert Spitzer, S.J., Ph.D. and his colleagues at the Magis Institute. In Rev. Spitzer's brilliant, highly researched book, *The Soul's Upward Yearning*, he quotes Nobel Prize awarded Australian neurophysiologist, Sir John Eccles: *"I am forced to accept the supernatural creation of the unique, spiritual, and personal 'I' – that is, the soul. Or, to put it in theological terms, every Soul is a new Divine creation unfused into the human embryo."*

[14] Saint Louis de Montfort, Treatise, *The Secret of the Rosary* (Bay Shore, NJ: Montfort Fathers, 1954).

[15] Denis, Gabriel, S.M.M, *The Reign of Jesus Through Mary*, Revised Edition, (Bayshore, NY: Montfort Publications, 1983), pp 41-45.

[16] John 19:27

[17] See Endnote 2, *Meetings with Mary op. cit.*, pp 94-101.

[18] Matthew 25:31-46

[19] John 3:15-16, 6:4, 10:28, 17:3

[20] Luke 2:7

[21] Matthew 25:34

## AUTHOR'S NOTE

[1] *Magnificat,* September 5, 2020, Vol.22, No. 7, p. 73.

[2] Prayer written by Saint Theresa of Calcutta for this work.

Made in the USA
Las Vegas, NV
25 June 2021